JOHN HAGEE

PROMISE
PROBLEM
PROVISION

A 40-DAY JOURNEY
TOWARD YOUR PROMISE

GOOSE CREEK
PUBLISHING

ISBN: 978-1-951701-25-3

Assembled and Produced for Goose Creek Publishing by Breakfast for Seven
2150 E. Continental Blvd., Southlake, TX 76092.

Printed in the United States of America.

SECTION 1:
PROMISE

SECTION 2:
PROBLEM

SECTION 3:
PROVISION

DISCOVER JUST HOW MUCH GOD IS WILLING TO KEEP HIS PROMISES TO YOU.

This 40-day devotional is a collection of principles that will reveal to you a supernatural plan that can open the windows of Heaven, pour out blessings you can't contain, and help you solve every problem you have for the rest of your life.

When you apply these truths to your problems, you will gain the ability to transform your earthly problems into divine provision. You will learn how to obtain wells you didn't dig, houses you didn't build, and vineyards you didn't plant. You will discover how you can dramatically improve your marriage, your mental health, your business, and light a rocket under your potential for personal success.

If you're ready to allow God to work in you, His supernatural peace can be yours all the days of your life. He will never leave you and He holds your hand while you walk through even the most treacherous of valleys. You can find God's promises and His provision for you if you will only seek after Him, obey what He tells you to do, and maintain an attitude of praise.

God is a Good Shepherd who is willing to lead you through the wilderness and into the green pastures and still waters. You can learn how to keep your eyes on the prize and not look to the left or the right on your journey of life. When you follow the steps ordered by the Lord, your life can be like days of Heaven on earth, and you will inherit the promised land that the Lord has for you.

God has a promised land for your life, and there is something He wants to do in your business, in your home, and in your marriage. The Bible says, *"For I know the plans I have for you,"* declares the Lord, *"plans to prosper you and not to harm you, plans to give you hope and a future"* (Jeremiah 29:11, NIV). As a beloved child of God and a co-heir with Jesus, you can receive every promise from Heaven.

Over the next 40 days, you are invited to seek God's will, lift your voice in highest praise, and trust God to bring you into the provision that He has for your life. As you give praise to the Lord, walk in obedience to what He has called you to do, and honor Him for the good things in your life, doors will begin to open for you, and you will find the steps you need to take to move out of the wilderness.

You don't have to make a career out of your problem. Your story does not have to be that you spent 40 years wandering around a mountain in the wilderness before you reached the prize that God had for you. You can change your life and you can change your future. As you seek God's will and follow His Word, you can move out of the desert, cross the Jordan, and receive your inheritance from the Lord.

Let God lead you in the Way everlasting. When you do, you will find that there is abundant peace available to you along the journey of life. As you live a life of praise and keep your trust in the promises of God, you will find that God will give you the desires of your heart and blessings you cannot contain. God knows your every need and He has a perfect plan for your life. You can believe and stand in faith for His provision right where you are.

Regardless of your current circumstances, God will never leave you nor forsake you. Learn to lean on Him in everything you do and fill your heart and mind with the Word of God. You can enter into the promised land of provision that God has for your life and you can inherit the good destiny and fulfilled purpose that He has in mind for you.

Let the next 40 days of reading *Promise, Problem, Provision* become a sacred time apart in prayer, Bible study, and worship. Know that in Christ, your redemption ever draweth nigh. Purpose in your heart to spend some time in prayer and come away with the Lord. As you draw near to hear from Him, you will discover how to follow His lead as you leave the wilderness and walk into God's promised land for you.

PART ONE

PROMISE

GREAT PROMISES

God gives great promises and keeps great promises. If you want to receive great things from God, you've first got to see Him for who He is. You've got to fix your eyes on the King of Kings and the Lord of Lords. He is the Alpha and the Omega, He is the Beginning and the End, He is God Almighty, and nothing under Heaven or earth is impossible for Him.

He owns the cattle on a thousand hills. He created the mountains and the seas. He spoke the world into existence. He is seated upon a throne in Heaven, surrounded by myriads of angels and enthroned in power and great glory. He is the one who can give great promises to His people. And when you receive a promise from God, remember that nothing is impossible for Him. He is the Great King of all the Universe.

There is something you need to know about promises you receive from Almighty God. The greater the promise, the greater the problem you will have to overcome. Those who receive incredible promises from the courts of Heaven must first overcome incredible problems before they receive incredible provision.

It is a truth for the ages: the greater the promise, the greater the problem. If God gives you a million-dollar promise, He will give you a million-dollar problem. We see this throughout the Scriptures and with the saints of old, through whom God worked mighty exploits both in the Old and New Testaments.

Before Abraham received the promise that God would make him into a great nation, he first had to leave his home and family and go to a land that God would show him. Before Joseph became second in command over all of Egypt, he was sold as a slave and wrongly imprisoned.

Before David was crowned king over Israel and given a 40-year reign, he had to run for his life in the wilderness as a vagabond. Before Jesus ascended into Heaven and sat down at the right hand of God, He went to the Cross.

We like million-dollar promises and ten-dollar problems, but it doesn't work that way. If you have a million-dollar promise, rest assured that you will have to overcome a million-dollar problem. The key to achieving your million-dollar promise will be learning how to meet your problems, overcome each one, and inherit God's divine provision.

APPLICATION

Do you have a million-dollar problem? Jeremiah 33:3 (NKJV) says, *"Call to Me, and I will answer you, and show you great and mighty things, which you do not know."* Call on the Lord today. Ask Him to show you the things you can do today to take steps through your problem and towards His provision.

REACTING TO YOUR PROBLEM

Problems are a normal part of life, and they are a normal part of being a Christian. There is nothing wrong with you if you are going through a problem. All throughout the Bible, we see God's people, prophets, priests, and kings, going through problems. Problems are normal.

The supernatural principle you need to learn is how to transform your problems into God's divine provision. How you react to your problems is what will determine your trajectory for success in your marriage, your health, your business, and every area of your life.

Your reaction to your problems will mark the difference between circling the same mountain of defeat for years or receiving your inheritance from God. Will you be crushed by the setbacks you have experienced and stay knocked down? Or will you rise up, shake the dust off your boots, and lift a mighty shout of praise? Victory is ever within your reach, but it rests on the wings of praise.

It is a clear Biblical principle. How you react to your problem will determine how long you stay in your problem. If you meet your problem head-on, pray and seek God for a solution, and do what He tells you to do, you will pass through your problem and move into your promised land.

However, if you only talk about your problems, only lament about your problems, only sit back and pout about your problems, you will be stuck with your problems for years to come. It's up to you. You can stay defined by your problems for life, or you can pass through them and receive God's provision.

The Israelites stayed in the wilderness for 40 years. A trek that should have only taken two weeks ended up taking them four decades because they were more focused on the problems they heard about from 10 spies than on God's promise of deliverance. Fear of the unknown and unbelief in God's Word kept an entire generation from inheriting the land of milk and honey.

In contrast, Jesus spent 40 days in the wilderness. The Bible says He was led there by the Spirit. In those deserted places, He was alone, hungry, and exposed to the elements. After those 40 days, He was in a weakened state. But even then, He chose to focus on the Word of God rather than the smooth words of compromise from the devil.

Jesus did not end up in the wilderness due to sin. He did not end up alone in the desert because of poor choices, disobedience, or punishment from God. No. The Bible says, *"Jesus was led up by the Spirit into the wilderness"* (Matthew 4:1, NKJV). The majority of people don't see that the problem Jesus had to overcome came from God. In the wilderness, He was tempted by the devil, and in the wilderness, He overcame him by the Word of God.

How you react to the problems in your life will determine your future, define your destiny, and decide whether you spend the majority of your life in the wilderness or in your promised land. The choice lies with you and how you react to the problems that stand between you and God's provision.

APPLICATION

How can you begin reacting to your problems the way God would have you react? Ask Him for faith. Ask Him for His perspective. Ask Him for wisdom to know how to react (James 1:5).

KEEP YOUR EYE ON THE PROMISE

The majority of people fail to see the problems in their lives as sent from God. If you view every problem as a punishment, you can easily become bitter and resentful. If you believe that every problem you face is because of your own shortcomings, then when you face a problem, you will complain, whine, and murmur. If that is how you view problems, you will live in an endless cycle of returning to the same problems over and over.

Don't make a career out of your problem. Your problems don't define you. Just because you are in a problem, or have a very large problem, or even have a whole host of problems, don't give into making those problems your identity for life. You are not your problems.

You've got to keep your eye on the promise that is past the problem. You've got to remember that your redemption draweth nigh. No matter what, you've got to get back up and keep moving forward. The quickest way through a problem is straight through it. Lift your eyes to the hills again. Whatever problem has come your way, remember that your help comes from the Lord.

In the middle of your problem, look to the promise. Look to the Word. Find God's promises for healing of your heart, of your body, and of your marriage. Nothing is too difficult for God. Keep working towards the success of your business, and don't stop fighting for the restoration of your family. You can inherit your promised land just like the Israelites did if you keep your heart in the Word of God and your eyes on His good promises.

Don't quit and don't give up. There is always hope. Contend for a rebirth of hope for your future. When your eyes are fixed on Jesus, your problems will begin to get smaller and smaller. Nothing is impossible for God. There is no mountain too high, there is no valley too deep, and there is no problem too insurmountable for the greatness, power, and majesty of God Most High.

Look today to the Author of your faith. Return your gaze to the One who created the universe and holds the stars in His right hand. He Himself is your promise for good and your exceeding great reward. As you draw near to Him, He will draw near to you. He is your Good Shepherd.

Do not let the problems in your life take first place in your mind, your thoughts, or your emotions. Look unto Jesus once more. In Him you will find the prosperity of wells you didn't dig, the harvest of vineyards you didn't plant, and the dwelling of houses you did not build. Today, and every day, keep your eye on the promises of God and your hope fixed on Him.

APPLICATION

What problem is on the forefront of your mind right now? Pray and submit that specific problem to God in Heaven. Let your hope arise once more as you set your mind on Him. Isaiah 26:3–4 tells us: *"You will keep him in perfect peace, whose mind is stayed on You, because he trusts in You. Trust in the* LORD *forever, for in* YAH, *the* LORD, *is everlasting strength"* (NKJV).

ISRAEL OWNS THE LAND

In Genesis 17, God made a covenant with Abraham regarding a specific piece of real estate on the earth. God looked out over the world He had created, and He chose a land with detailed borders that He would give as an inheritance to His people. Then He made a covenant with Abraham that his descendants would inherit that land, the land of Israel.

"And I will establish My covenant between Me and you and your descendants after you in their generations, for an everlasting covenant, to be God to you and your descendants after you. Also

I give to you and your descendants after you the land in which you are a stranger, all the land of Canaan, as an everlasting possession; and I will be their God" (Genesis 17:7–8, NKJV).

God made a covenant that He would give the land of Israel to Abraham in Genesis 17:7–8. The promise of the land was then passed to Isaac in Genesis 26:2–5. Finally, God made a third promise to Jacob, who would become known as Israel, in Genesis 28:10–15. It is clear in Scripture that God left no doubt as to who the land of Israel would be given to — the descendants of Abraham, Isaac, and Jacob.

When God makes a covenant, He keeps His word. No word that God has ever spoken has fallen to the ground or returned void. God promised the land of Canaan, the land of Israel, as an everlasting inheritance to His people and to His people alone. Today, and forever, the land of Israel belongs to the people of Israel.

The Jewish people have received great and mighty promises from God in Scripture. In Romans 9, Paul wrote of his people, "*...my brethren, my countrymen according to the flesh, who are Israelites, to whom pertain the adoption, the glory, the covenants, the giving of the law, the service of God, and the promises; of whom are the fathers and from* *whom, according to the flesh, Christ came, who is over all, the eternally blessed God. Amen"* (Romans 9:3–5, NKJV).

The Jewish people received incredible promises from God. They have also endured some of the most difficult problems of any people throughout the entirety of history. The Jews, God's chosen people, more so than any other people, have endured threats, danger, and violence for thousands of years, dispersed among the nations of the world. They have lived through expulsions, persecutions, the Inquisition, Pogroms, the Holocaust, and the scourge of antisemitism.

Yet, they have overcome. Modern-day Israel is a modern-day miracle. The land of Israel is now the provision of God according to the promise of God for the people of God. Against all odds, the Jewish people arose from the ashes of the Holocaust, defeated invading armies, and built the Promised Land of Israel into one of the most dynamic, industrious, and beautiful countries on the world stage today.

APPLICATION

As we understand more of God's heart and plan for Israel, we will also come to understand more about God. How does God speak about Israel in the Bible? Ask the Lord that you might see Israel and the Jewish people the way He does. Spend time in prayer over the Scriptures concerning Israel, Jerusalem, and the Jewish people.

---

40 YEARS

When God spoke to Moses to go to Pharaoh in Egypt and tell him to "Let My people go," it marked the beginning of an incredible time of history for the Jewish people. For over 400 years, they had been in bondage to the Egyptians. Generations had come and gone, lived and died, all under the oppression and slavery of Pharaoh. But through the power of the 10 plagues, God took the Jewish people out of Egypt. He delivered them from bondage, from slavery, and from Pharaoh — who was a type of the enemy as he wore a serpent's crown.

But God sent Israel a deliverer in Moses, and they walked out of slavery once and for all. God took them out of Egypt, and they would never return again. However, they were still in chains in many other ways. Though free in body, they were still in bondage in their minds and souls.

They rebelled against God in the wilderness and would not believe the report of Joshua and Caleb that they were well able to take the Promised Land of Israel. Because of their reaction to their problem, and because of their unbelief, they would spend 40 years wandering in the wilderness.

God took the Jewish people out of Egypt. That's a type of deliverance, deliverance because they were slaves and owned by Pharaoh. Then God took them through the Red Sea. That means He took them through water, which is a type of water baptism. And then He took them into the wilderness, which is a type of problem.

For 40 years, they took laps around the wilderness. They went around Mount Sinai again and again, going in circles around the mountain. Are you going around the same mountains? Are you taking laps around the same problems? Five years go by and you're in the same place. Don't confuse motion with progress. What has the Lord asked you to do? You need to get serious about diligently obeying the voice of God.

After 40 years, they reached the Promised Land, which was their provision. To this day, the Jewish people own the land of Israel by blood covenant with God Almighty. The lesson here is that the quickest way to overcome a problem is to go straight through it. They could have walked straight through the wilderness in two weeks, but it took them 40 years to reach the Promised Land. It took God one day to get Israel out of Egypt, but it took 40 years to get Egypt out of Israel.

An entire generation died in the wilderness. They died in the wilderness because they did not react the right way to their problem. Don't make the problem your career, your identity, or who you are. Don't wrestle with the same problem for 20 years. You are not your problem. You are not your past.

Do yourself a favor and forget your past. Your past is history, and your future is a mystery. Today is the gift of God. That's why they call it the present. Live today to the glory of God with love, joy, and peace, knowing that you're marching to the prize that God has prepared for you.

APPLICATION

What has the Lord asked you to do? What dream has He put on your heart? If you get serious and write out a step-by-step plan with bite-size goals, you will make progress moving out of the problem and into His provision for you.

THE PROBLEM THAT INFURIATES YOU

Problems are normal. Everyone is either coming out of a problem, going through a problem, or about to have a problem. In John 16:33, Jesus said "...*In the world you will have tribulation; but be of good cheer, I have overcome the world*" (NKJV). Problems are an important part of life because God will put you in a problem to show you what is in you.

Problems also help you focus. If you're wondering what God put you on the planet for, think about the problems that infuriate you. Not everyone thinks about the same problems that you do. Jim Elliot saw that the Waorani people in Ecuador had not heard of Jesus. He and four other missionaries ultimately gave their lives for the sake of the Gospel. [i] In the 1800s, William Wilberforce fought for years for the abolition of the slave trade across the British Empire. [ii] The problem that infuriates you the most is the problem God has assigned you to solve.

David Livingstone, the Scottish missionary who spent his life's strength in Africa in the 1800s, was so committed to his cause that when he died, his body was carried back to England, but his heart was buried under a mpundu tree in what is now modern-day Zambia. To this day, his tombstone in Westminster Abbey speaks of his commitment and is inscribed in stone with these words: *"All I can add in my solitude, is, may Heaven's rich blessing come down on every one, American, English, or Turk, who will help to heal this open sore of the world."* [iii]

Your problem can lead you to your destiny. The problem that infuriated Moses was Egypt's enslavement of the Jewish people. Moses was so impassioned by the injustice that he killed an Egyptian who was whipping a Jewish slave. Even while still a prince of Egypt, Moses' heart was moved for his people. But the problem was that he tried to fulfill in the flesh what only God could do supernaturally.

God enrolled Moses in the University of Adversity. He sent Moses into the wilderness as a shepherd for 40 years to prepare him for his true destiny.

The wilderness was a problem for Moses that he did not foresee. In one day, Moses went from being a son of the palace to being a pauper in the desert. He went from royal robes and servants at his beck and call to the bleating of animals, shepherd's rags, and the stench of sheep. Yet it was in the wilderness that Moses received the power he needed from God to liberate all of Israel from slavery. This is a much greater feat than he could ever do on his own.

Consider that the problems that you currently have are actually sent by God, ordained by God, and approved by God — and that it's all for your good. In the wilderness, Moses learned to hear God's voice. On the back side of the desert, he learned to walk and talk with God. Exodus 33:11 tells us *"The Lord would speak to Moses face to face, as one speaks to a friend"* (NIV).

APPLICATION

What is the problem that infuriates you? What problem do you think about over and over? What keeps coming up in your life, no matter where you turn? The problem that you see, and that you seek to resolve, could very well lead you straight into your destiny.

DAY 07
MARAH

The children of Israel who left Egypt witnessed some of the greatest miracles the world had ever seen. They saw God work signs and wonders through the 10 plagues. They were the first generation in 430 years to be set free from bondage, and they were the ones who walked through the Red Sea on dry ground, following a cloud by day and a fire by night.

But what happened right after they crossed the Red Sea? A problem. Right after a major victory comes a major trial. Where was the first place God led Israel? Straight to the bitter waters of Marah. Marah means bitter in Hebrew, and He took them there to introduce them to a problem to find out what's inside them.

Only three days earlier, they had been dancing on the banks of water where they had seen their enemies dead on the shore. Only 72 hours ago, they had lifted up shouts of joy and praise because of the great victory that God had just worked in their lives. And now, three days later, hot and thirsty in the desert, they find undrinkable, bitter water.

God took them to Marah to test them, to see what was on the inside of their hearts. Would they serve Him? Would they rise in faith? Would they believe that just as He delivered them from the hand of their Egyptian masters, He would also deliver them from thirst in the desert? God will not use anyone until they go through His blast furnace, until He tests them with problems, trials, and difficulty. How do you act when you get to the first problem on the other side of a great victory? You walk into your house, you don't even know you've got a marriage problem, and your spouse says, "I want a divorce." You go to work in the morning, you think everything is fine, and your boss says, "You're fired."

You go to the doctor for a little bump on your foot, but the doctor says, "It's cancer."

What do you do when tragedy strikes like lightning out of the clear blue sky? How do you act then? Remember, how you react in the problem determines how long you stay in the problem. When you're in the fight for your life, will you stay in faith and lift your voice in praise? Or will you sink into despair, murmuring, and complaining, and keep talking about your problem for years on end?

You don't know what you're made of until you go through the fire. Steel is tested by fire, soldiers are tested by combat, and the saints of God are tested by fiery trials and problems. 1 Peter 4:12–13 says, *"Beloved, do not think it strange concerning the fiery trial which is to try you, as though some strange thing happened to you; but rejoice to the extent that you partake of Christ's sufferings, that when His glory is revealed, you may also be glad with exceeding joy"* (NKJV).

You may not believe that God sends you problems, but the truth is that He most certainly does. He will send you problems to grow you and mature you into who He has created you to be. Problems are normal and God gives us problems to force us to examine ourselves and discover His will for our lives.

APPLICATION

Are you drawing near to God in your problems, or are you drawing away? Write down the problems you are experiencing in life right now and ask God what He wants you to learn through them today.

THE POTTER'S HAND

Years ago, Diana and I were in Israel visiting the Holy Land. During the trip, we went to a potter's house in Hebron. It was as though we had stepped back in time and into the pages of Scripture. We found ourselves standing in a room watching a potter making pottery just like they made in the days of Jeremiah.

He had a wheel driven by a foot pedal, a spinning table on top, and piles of clay all around. He began with an idea in his mind and a simple lump of clay from the pile. That clay would represent you and me. He threw that lump of clay on the wheel, and he began to shape it. After he spun the clay for a while, he would stop it from spinning and smash the lumps out of the clay. Over and over, he kept working on that clay. He took the clay and would whack it with his hand. You'd almost jump every time he hit the clay. He crushed every possible lump out, so it would be pliable for the spinning wheel. That's what God does to us.

The potter continued to crush the clay to shape it into the form he desired. God only uses molded people, yielded people, those who have been on the potter's wheel. It's broken things that God uses. It is broken ground that produces the harvest. It is a broken grape that produces new wine. It was a broken alabaster box that was used to anoint Jesus before the Cross.

In the hands of the potter, the vessel began to take shape. And when all the lumps were out, all the imperfections were smooth, and it was in a perfectly molded shape, that little vessel probably said, "Ah, it's finally over. All of my lumps are out, and now I'm through. The potter is done with me, and I can rest." But that was when the potter took that vessel, put it in a roaring fire, and shut the door.

"How long are you going to leave it in there?" I asked. "Until it turns cherry red," he answered. "How do you know you've left it in there long enough?" He said, "In a few minutes, I will open the door, take it out, and hold it in my hand. I will thump it on the edge. When I thump it, if it sings, I know it's ready."

If God has molded you and shaped you, if He has put you in the fire and closed the door, if He is now holding you in His hand and you feel a thump on the side, lift a shout of praise to God! Lift your voice and start singing. Praise and thanksgiving are the shortcuts through the times of testing. Problems are normal. The spinning wheel, the smoothing of imperfections, and even the blazing fire of the kiln are all part of God's plan.

APPLICATION

Are you going through a trial right now? The quickest way through is to give God highest praise. Praise, worship, and thanksgiving will open the door for you just like it did for Paul and Silas in that Philippian jail (Acts 16:25–26). Write down some areas in your life over which you can pray, sing, and lift your voice in praise.

FASCINATION, FORM, FACT

Adam and Eve lived in the definition of paradise. The Garden of Eden had no pain, no regret, and no danger of any kind. There were no thorns on the trees, no stickers hiding in the grass, and they couldn't even get a sunburn. Adam and Eve walked with God throughout the garden every day and enjoyed perfect communion with Him.

The promise that they had was fellowship with God. They walked and talked together and enjoyed the company of Almighty God. They had everything that they needed to live in a perfect paradise with neither shame nor fear.

But along came a problem. In Genesis 3, Satan tempted Eve with the fruit of the forbidden tree. It began with fascination. *"Has God indeed said..."* (v. 1). Satan began his temptation. *"You will not surely die"* (v. 4). When Eve listened to his voice, her heart became fascinated with the forbidden fruit. *"So when the woman saw that the tree was good for food, that it was pleasant to the eyes, and a tree desirable to make one wise, she took of its fruit and ate"* (Genesis 3:6, NKJV).

She became fascinated with what she did not have and with what she did not know. Before she ever reached out her hand to pick that fruit, her eyes were fascinated with how it looked, and her heart was enraptured with what she believed it would do for her. Because of her fascination with the forbidden, she gave into the words of the serpent.

Fascination led to form. She reached out her hand. She plucked the fruit off the vine. She held it, looked at it, saw that it was pleasant to the eyes, and took that bite. When Adam and Eve ate from that tree, the form of the fruit led to the fact of sin. The fact was that they were now in total rebellion. They failed in the problem and were driven out into the wilderness. Their provision was exile.

You need to understand that when you fail in the problem, your family will feel the pain with you. You don't feel it by yourself; it spreads like a pebble dropped in a pond, and the ripples of every decision fan out in every direction for years to come. Everything you do affects the people around you.

Great sin can begin with simple fascination. When fascination takes hold of your heart, it becomes a form. When you reach out your hand and grasp that form, it becomes fact. Romans 6:23 says, *"For the wages of sin is death, but the gift of God is eternal life in Christ Jesus our Lord"* (NKJV). All Eve had to say was, "Look, I don't talk to strange snakes when my husband's not home." It would've never been a problem, but Adam and Eve got kicked out of the Garden of Eden because they failed in the problem, and all of humanity lives with the effects of their decision to this day.

APPLICATION

Are there any places in your heart that you have given way to fascination with the forbidden? Today is the day of repentance and today is the day of salvation. Give your heart fully to the Lord and ask Him to show you any areas that you need to commit fully to Him. *"You shall love the*

LORD your God with all your heart, with all your soul, and with all your strength" (Deuteronomy 6:5, NKJV).

DAY 10

PROMISES, PROMISES

There are more than 3,000 promises in the Bible. The promises in the Word of God are more valuable than a certificate of deposit that you can put in your bank and more valuable than all the wealth in the entire world. If you want to succeed in life, you must learn to stand on the promises of God. The Bible is the solid rock for your soul and your shelter in the time of the storm. These promises can open the gates of Heaven and close the gates of Hell. They are precious, they are powerful, they are personal, they are proven. Build your life on the promises of the Word of God and they will never fail you.

Everything God offers you comes in promise form. James 1:17 says, *"Every good gift and every perfect gift is from above, and comes down from the Father of lights, with whom there is no variation or shadow of turning"* (NKJV). God is the Great Giver of every good gift. Salvation is a promise. In Genesis 3:15 we read, *"I will put enmity between you and the woman, and between your offspring and hers; he will crush your head, and you will strike his heel"* (NIV). Thousands of years later, that Scripture was fulfilled when Satan's head was crushed at the Cross. To this day, he is a defeated foe, and his legions tremble at the mention of Jesus' name. The victory is ours forever through Christ the Lord. And *"Everyone who calls on the name of the Lord will be saved"* (Romans 10:13, NIV).

Prosperity is a promise. After Moses died, God spoke to Joshua and commissioned him as the leader of Israel and said, *"This Book of the Law shall not depart from your mouth, but you shall meditate in it day and night, that you may observe to do according to all that is written in it. For then you will make your way prosperous, and then you will have good success"* (Joshua 1:8, NKJV). And again, in the New Testament, John wrote, *"Beloved, I pray that you may prosper in all things and be in health, just as your soul prospers*" (3 John 1:2, NKJV). You have a Biblical right to expect prosperity if you live a righteous life!

The Psalmist wrote: "*Blessed is the man who walks not in the counsel of the ungodly, nor stands in the path of sinners, nor sits in the seat of the scornful; but his delight is in the law of the LORD, and in His law he meditates day and night. He shall be like a tree planted by the rivers of water, that brings forth its fruit in its season, whose leaf also shall not wither; and whatever he does shall prosper*" (Psalm 1:1–3, NKJV). The promises of God are a gold mine for every Believer. All they are waiting for is for you to open the Book.

Healing is a promise. After the crossing of the Red Sea, God said to the Israelites: "*If you diligently heed the voice of the LORD your God and do what is right in His sight, give ear to His commandments and keep all His statutes, I will put none of the diseases on you which I have brought on the Egyptians. For I am the LORD who heals you*" (Exodus 15:26, NKJV). And Isaiah prophesied that healing would come through the Messiah: "*But He was wounded for our transgressions, He was bruised for our iniquities; the chastisement for our peace was upon Him, and by His stripes we are healed*" (Isaiah 53:5, NKJV). And again, the Psalmist wrote: "*Bless the LORD, O my soul, and forget not all His benefits: who forgives all your iniquities, who heals all your diseases"* (Psalm 103:2–3, NKJV).

APPLICATION

The promises of God are "Yes" in Christ (2 Corinthians 1:20). As a child of God, you can come boldly to the throne of grace and obtain mercy and grace to help in your time of need. What is on your mind today? Make a list of the needs in your life and write a Scripture reference across from each one. With prayer and thanksgiving, present your requests to God.

A RIGHT WAY AND A WRONG WAY

This is how the principle of promise, problem, and provision works in your life. God gives you a promise. It's a word from Him, it's a knowing in your spirit, it's a passage from Scripture. You look at the promise and you are full of faith that God will make a way where there is no way. But you have to remember that with every promise, there is a problem in the middle, before you reach the provision.

The problem is the bridge between the promise and the provision. The problem is the process you go through before you receive all that God has for you. How long you stay in the problem is entirely up to you. You can circle the mountain once, or you can keep making laps for the rest of your life. There is a right way and a wrong way to respond to your problem.

Here's the wrong way: if every time a problem comes into your life, your first response is to complain about it, to whine about it, to talk to everyone else except God about it, chances are you'll stay in that problem for the foreseeable future.

If you always say things like: "Nothing good ever happens to me. Poor, poor me. I'm just going to go out in the garden and eat worms. If I inherited General Motors, someone would outlaw cars. The only way to wake up with a smile on your face in this dog-eat-dog world is to go to bed at night with a coat hanger in your mouth. I'm just stuck forever." An attitude like that will keep you stuck in your problem for the rest of your life.

Here's the right way: you recognize that problems come from God and that problems are not bad. A problem in your life does not mean that you are living outside of the will of God. A problem in your life could very well be proof that God is working in you and is trying to grow you and mature you to be more like Christ.

So, when a problem comes your way, your first and immediate response needs to be that you draw nearer to God than ever before (James 4:8). Let your knees be found knelt in prayer, your voice lifted to Heaven, and your heart filled with praise to God Most High. Praise and thanksgiving will open doors for you faster than almost anything else you can do.

When your heart is right before Him, God can promote you to the provision that He has for you. When your heart is filled with praise and thanksgiving, even in the valley of the shadow of death, all your attention moves away from your own strength or self-sufficiency, and your hope is set on Jesus Christ alone. Praise recalibrates your heart to the Prince of Peace. When your eyes are fixed on things above (Colossians 3:2) and your heart is set on a better country — a Heavenly one — you open the door to move out of the problem and into the provision.

APPLICATION

Are there any areas of your life that you have given way to murmuring, complaining, or unbelief in the promises of

God? Take some time to come away with God. Let Him speak kindly and reassuringly to your heart once again. Write out your praise and thanksgiving to God.

_____

_____

_____

_____

_____

_____

_____

_____

_____

_____

_____

_____

_____

_____

_____

_____

_____

_____

_____

_____

_____

DREAMER OF DREAMS

Jacob loved his son Joseph because he was the son of his favorite wife, Rachel. Jacob favored Joseph over his 11 brothers and even gave him a hot sport coat, a coat of many colors. When Joseph was only a teenager, he had some incredible dreams from God and shared them with his brothers and his father.

His dreams were his promise from God. In one dream, he saw his brothers' sheaves of grain bowing down to his sheaf of grain. In another, he said, *"the sun and moon and eleven stars were bowing down to me"* (Genesis 37:9, NIV).

On top of these dreams of greatness, his brothers knew their father loved him the most, and they hated him for it. They cast him into a pit, faked his death, and sold him into slavery.

Now Joseph had a problem. Lowest of the low and a slave in a foreign land to a foreign master, Joseph's dreams of greatness were only a memory. But what did he do? He faithfully served God as best he could, right where he was. But there in Potiphar's house, Potiphar's wife started making eyes at him and tried to seduce him. When he refused, she accused him of accosting her and Potiphar threw Joseph in prison.

Now even lower than before, he was not only a slave, but a slave bound to prison for about 12 years. It looked like he was a million miles away from the will of God. But the Lord was with him. In prison, he met Pharaoh's baker and cupbearer, who told Pharaoh about Joseph. And in one day, God moved Joseph from the prison to the palace and used him to save all of Egypt and Israel in the midst of one of the greatest famines the world had known.

When Joseph was in prison, everybody who knew him would have said, "Surely, he has to be out of the will of

God. He's been in jail for years, and even his brothers rejected him. He's been thrown in here by one of the most prominent families in all of Egypt. Who could he possibly be?" But Joseph was never closer to God in all his life than when he was in that prison. Even there, in a dark and forgotten cistern, he was in the middle of God's will. The Bible says that the Lord was with him and gave him favor in the eyes of the jailkeeper. Joseph did not wallow in self-pity; he got to work. The reason Joseph got out of that prison was because of how he reacted in the middle of his problem.

God took him out of the pit and established him in the palace. He gave him the keys of Egypt, and he became the most powerful man on the face of the whole earth, with only the exception of Pharaoh. Joseph saved the gentile world from starvation and made it possible for the Jewish people to be saved as well. Thousands of years later, Jesus Christ would come through the Jewish people and save the whole world.

One boy went through a problem that was hell on earth. In the middle of the problem, his reaction was to continually turn to God. He moved through his problem and straight into a provision that exceeded his hopes and dreams. Joseph passed the test, and you can too.

APPLICATION

How you react in the middle of your problems today will not only determine your destiny, but the destiny of your family tree. What adjustments do you need to make in your life so that you pass through your problems and inherit the provision that God has for you?

THE PROVISION OF CHRIST

Consider the promise, problem, and provision of Jesus Christ. Consider He who is the greatest of all. The One who was foretold as the coming Messiah for thousands of years. The One who bled, died, and rose again. The One who rules and reigns in Heaven as the Alpha and the Omega, the First and the Last, the Beginning and the End. Jesus Christ, who was given the promise to be the Savior of the world.

Mary saw Him as an infant in Bethlehem's manger. John the Baptist saw Him as a candidate for baptism in the

Jordan River. The disciples saw Him as a Jewish rabbi and a great teacher. Rome saw Him as an insurrectionist, too dangerous to live. The Pharisees saw Him as a heretic. But one day, we shall see Him for who He is. And when we do, we shall see Him as King of Kings and Lord of Lords, the fairest of 10,000, the Lion of the tribe of Judah, and the Bright and Morning Star.

The problem that Jesus overcame was the Cross. The problem for the Prince of Heaven was that He had to pay the price for the sins of the world. For you and for me. *"He is despised and rejected by men, a Man of sorrows and acquainted with grief. And we hid, as it were, our faces from Him; He was despised, and we did not esteem Him. Surely He has borne our griefs and carried our sorrows; yet we esteemed Him stricken, smitten by God, and afflicted. But He was wounded for our transgressions, He was bruised for our iniquities; the chastisement for our peace was upon Him, and by His stripes we are healed"* (Isaiah 53:3–5, NKJV).

There at Calvary, He conquered hell, death, and the grave. In one day, He disarmed the powers and authorities, making a public spectacle of them and triumphing over them at the Cross (Colossians 2:15). And on that great day, the day of our salvation, the day the sun was darkened, and the earth shook, He accomplished everything He was sent to do and said, *"It is finished"* (John 19:30, NIV).

And on Easter morning, He rose from the grave! In Revelation 1:18 (NIV), He says, *"I am the Living One; I was dead, and now look, I am alive for ever and ever! And I hold the keys of death and Hades."* No longer the suffering servant, He is the Great I Am, the Shepherd of the Church, and God Immanuel. He crushed Satan's head and was given a name above every other name. He is Heaven's hope and Hell's dread.

He has all power in Heaven and earth. He rose from the dead in the city of Jerusalem, and He's coming back again. We will see Him coming on the clouds from Heaven with great power and majesty. The King of all, surrounded with all power and great glory. He is coming back again. He will return to Jerusalem, announce Himself as Lord, and put His foot on the Mount of Olives. He's going to set up a Kingdom that will last forever. The King is coming back, full of grace and truth, and in power and great glory. And you can be a part of that Kingdom. Through faith in Christ, you too can dwell in the house of the Lord forever.

APPLICATION

Have you committed all of your heart, all of your mind, and all of your will to Jesus? Have you made Him supreme Lord over your heart and life? Today can be the day when you give your will, totally, to Jesus Christ. Call on the Name of the Lord and write out your prayer of allegiance to Him (John 10:9, Romans 10:9, Romans 10:13).

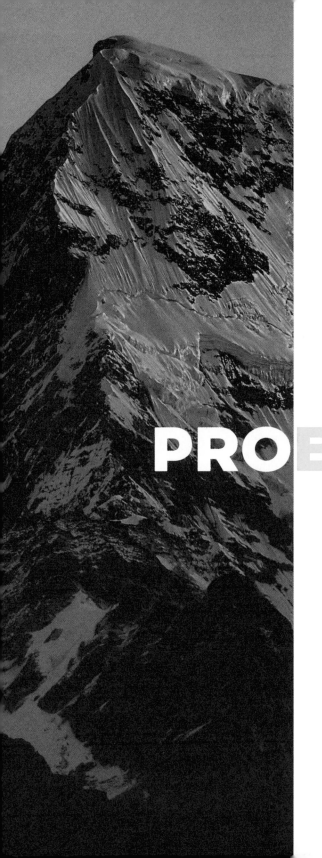

PART TWO

PROBLEM

DAY 14

FATHER ABRAHAM

Abraham is one of the foremost figures in the entire Bible. He is the father of all who believe and is known in the Bible as "God's friend." Few men who ever lived are as well known around the world and across the stage of history. To that end, Abraham received one of the greatest promises that God ever gave a man.

In what is known as the Abrahamic Covenant, God gave Abraham a promise that literally shaped the history of the world. The covenant that God made with him was unconditional and would bless his descendants from one generation to the next and the nations of the world.

In Genesis 12 we read: *"Get out of your country, from your family and from your father's house, to a land that I will show you. I will make you a great nation; I will bless you and make your name great; and you shall be a blessing. I will bless those who bless you, and I will curse him who curses you; and in you all the families of the earth shall be blessed"* (Genesis 12:1–3, NKJV).

God told Abraham that He would give him the land of Israel and make his name great. God said that He would bless those who bless him and curse those who curse him. God promised that He would bless all the nations of the earth through him. This was an incredible promise, and God will never go back on His word. However, the global promise to be the "father of many nations" also came with a big problem for Abraham to overcome.

What kind of a problem did he have? A global one. A big one. God told Abraham to leave his father, who worshiped idols, leave his land, and leave his family. Then, in Genesis 22:2, God tested him and said, *"Take your son, your only son, whom you love—Isaac—and go to the region of Moriah.*

Sacrifice him there as a burnt offering on a mountain I will show you" (NIV). The problem for Abraham was that he now needed to follow God to a place he had never been before and place his son of promise, Isaac, on the altar of sacrifice.

But Abraham was a man who believed God, and his faith was credited to him as righteousness. And through righteousness that comes by faith, Abraham believed God. Abraham hoped against hope and concluded that God was able to raise Isaac up, even from the dead, and his faith was made complete by what he did.

Abraham believed God, obeyed God, and received the provision of the promise from God. To this day, thousands of years later and all over the world, Abraham is honored and remembered. His name is highly respected and deeply loved because he obeyed God in the problem. And from this one man came descendants as numerous as the stars in the sky and as countless as the sand on the seashore. The greater the promise, the greater the problem.

APPLICATION

What promises have you received from God? What problems have arisen along the way? If you will go straight through your problem with unwavering faith like Abraham, you will receive the provision that God has for you. Read about Abraham's faith in Genesis 12, Genesis 22, Romans 4, Hebrews 11, and James 2. What can you apply to your life and your problems today?

DAY 15

DELAYED OBEDIENCE

Obedience to God is a vital component if you do not want to make a career out of your problem. One of the most powerful things you can do in life to get yourself out of the wilderness and start moving toward the hopes, dreams, and promises from God is to go back and do the last thing He told you to do.

If you find yourself walking in the same ruts, circling the same mountains, and facing the same problems year after year, chances are there is something God has asked you to do, but you haven't done it yet. And until you complete the last thing He told you to do, you will not receive another assignment to move on to the next.

You need to make it a priority in your life to be obedient to the last thing God told you to do. Delayed obedience is a sophisticated way of saying that you are in open rebellion to God. Until you want to solve the problem, you're not going to solve it. Until you want to live in obedience to God, you will make a career living in the wilderness.

The children of Israel were in the desert for 40 years because they had not obeyed the Lord (Joshua 5:6). An entire generation was buried in the sand because they were too stiff-necked to follow God in faith. You don't have to die in the wilderness. You can possess your promised land.

Don't make the same mistakes that Israel made. Don't only know about the Word of God, or speak highly of the Word of God, or even keep a Bible on your nightstand, but never obey what it tells you to do. If you want to live in the land that flows with milk and honey, which represents your business or personal success, you must organize your life in such a way that you live in obedience to the Word of God.

You don't have to live the rest of your life in a wilderness with your job, your relationships, or your dreams. Right now, and right where you are, determine that you will diligently obey the voice of the Lord. Motion is not progress. The only activity that matters for you is to get busy doing not a full list of good things, but the thing that God Himself has assigned for you.

Spend time in prayer and ask the Lord what is on His heart for you. What has He called you to do? Is it writing a book, starting a business, or planting a church? Do you feel the tug in your heart to move to the mission field, start a family, or reconcile with an old friend? The most important thing you can do today is that which God has asked you to do.

APPLICATION

Fill your heart and mind with the Word of God and your spirit will be more sensitive to the voice of the Lord. Make a list of the things the Lord has told you to do. As you walk in obedience, you will begin to feel the pleasure of the Lord and the favor of God upon the things you set your hand to do. What has God called you to do? What can you do today toward fulfilling that assignment?

DAY 16

THE PURPOSE
OF THE PROBLEM

Problems have purposes, and there is a purpose for every problem in your life. When problems come your way, if you keep your heart right before the Lord and draw near to Him instead of falling into self-pity, you will find that you will move through your problems as quickly as possible.

Every great man and woman of faith in the Bible had problems. The key is to remember that the purpose of the problem is to develop you. The problem is there to grow you, mature you, and spur you to draw nearer ever to your Lord. When Job was sitting in sackcloth and ashes after he lost all of his worldly possessions, even then, he kept his hope in the Lord. When David was running for his life across the desert from Saul, he kept praying and crying out to God. When Joseph was in prison in Egypt, he did not let his surroundings imprison his mind and thoughts. He kept looking to the Lord for deliverance.

Problems are resistance. When the Lord takes something away from your life, it's to give you something better. The story is told of the child who didn't want to go on a vacation to the beach because he couldn't see past the mudhole he was playing in in his own backyard. Intolerance of your present situation is the birthplace of your future. Sometimes, the purpose of the problem is to motivate you to a new level of accomplishment.

If you will stay close to the Master's hand and go straight through the problem, you can get to the land flowing with milk and honey pretty quickly. God wants you to have the best, but He also wants to have your heart. Nothing could be worse than getting to the land of God's provision and forgetting the Provider.

If God has taken you on a new adventure, quit living your life through a rear-view mirror. Remember that

God's ways are above your ways and His thoughts are above your thoughts. He loves you with an everlasting love and He always has your best in mind. If you'll trust Him and keep your eyes on the prize, He will lead you to green pastures and still waters.

He is the Great Shepherd, the One who leaves the ninety-nine to seek the one (Matthew 18:12), the Author and Finisher of your faith (Hebrews 12:2), and your Heavenly Father (Matthew 6:9). He is the One who gives promises, and He is the One who will take you into a problem to grow you, so that when you enter into His provision, you are able to keep and enjoy it.

Go through your problems today. You have not been left alone and you are in no way forgotten. Your God will never leave you nor forsake you. In any problem, you can be strong, be courageous, and strengthen yourself in the Lord. He is ever by your side — no more than a prayer away. Call on the Lord today and follow Him straight through the problem.

How have you been conducting yourself in the problem? The way you act in the problem determines how long you stay there. But if you will fill your mouth with praise, if you will draw near to God, if you will follow Him as a sheep follows a shepherd, He will lead you to the land of milk and honey.

APPLICATION

Are there any problems in your life that you need to redefine? What are some ways that you can draw near to God today?

DAY 17

GOD USES BROKEN THINGS

If you have ever experienced any level of brokenness in your life, I want you to know that God can take that broken thing and turn it into something beautiful. I want you to take heart about the brokenness in your past or the brokenness you may be going through right now, because God is in the business of using broken things.

Psalm 51:17 says, *"a broken and contrite heart you, God, will not despise"* (NIV). It takes broken soil to produce a crop. It takes broken clouds to give rain. It takes broken bread to produce strength. It was a broken alabaster box over the head of Jesus Christ that released the perfume that stayed with Him for the final 48 hours of His life. Peter denied Jesus three times on the night He was betrayed. He was left broken and weeping over his failure, yet the same Peter stood before the crowd on the day of Pentecost in Jerusalem and preached with such power that 3,000 people were saved.

When Jesus came out of the 40 days of testing in the wilderness, He returned to Galilee in the power of the Spirit. He went to the synagogue on the Sabbath, as was His custom, took the scroll and read from the book of Isaiah. In Isaiah 61:3, we read a portion of what Jesus read, *"To console those who mourn in Zion, to give them beauty for ashes, the oil of joy for mourning, the garment of praise for the spirit of heaviness; that they may be called trees of righteousness, the planting of the LORD, that He may be glorified"* (NKJV). If you look at your life and all you see are the ashes of old relationships, old hopes, and old dreams, look once more to Jesus. He is the One who can take those ashes and make something beautiful.

Take inventory of your heart. If you're honest, what do you find? Are you hard-hearted against the things of God? Do you pride yourself on being tougher than John Wayne? It's a dangerous thing to be calloused toward God and man. There is a principle at play here with regard to hearts that are hard. Hard hearts do not enter promised lands. Only clay that has been broken, smashed, spun, and fired in the kiln is turned into beautiful jars. Because God loves you, He will keep you in the problem until you crack, until your heart is soft toward the Lord, until you place King Jesus above King Self.

Here are two keys to remember. 1) God only uses broken things. 2) Praise opens the door for a breakthrough in your heart, which leads to a breakthrough in your life. Consider the words of Isaiah: *"Forget the former things; do not dwell on the past. See, I am doing a new thing! Now it springs up; do you not perceive it? I am making a way in the wilderness and streams in the wasteland. The wild animals honor me, the jackals and the owls, because I provide water in the wilderness and streams in the wasteland, to give drink to my people, my chosen, the people I formed for myself that they may proclaim my praise"* (Isaiah 43:18–21, NIV). God can make a way in the wilderness, bring water out of a rock, and cause streams to bubble up in the desert. Nothing is impossible for Him, but it is praise that opens the door, and a heart that is open to God that receives the promised provision.

APPLICATION

Do you have any parts of your heart that are hard toward God? Are you holding on to bitterness or anger toward yourself, toward someone you know, toward God? He already knows what's in your heart. What's important for you to do is get honest with God and with yourself. Write down the prayer that is on your heart today.

TAKE RESPONSIBILITY

One of the greatest lessons you will ever learn in life is that if you want to have any level of success, or make any sort of difference, you have to learn to take responsibility for your life and your actions. Do not become a member of the no-fault society that's sweeping America. You are like you are because you are what you are. It's called character. You are responsible for what you do. You are responsible for what you say. You are responsible for what you think. And if you're not responsible for your actions, you can never improve your life.

You will never make any progress towards the call of God on your life if you are always blaming someone else for your setbacks, mistakes, failures, or even times you missed the provision because you didn't have enough courage to step out. Not one ounce of good will ever come into your present life if you blame your parents, your coaches, your teachers, your friends, or anyone else who may have mistreated you, overlooked you, or forgotten about you.

There is One who has never let you down, never left you, never forsaken you, and never forgotten about you. There is One who has always been there, knows the hairs on your head (Luke 12:7), and knows the plans for good that He has for your life (Jeremiah 29:11). If you want to leave your past and move into your future, you need to forget the past and start spending your time thinking about your Heavenly Father who has, is, and will always be there for you.

There was once a mother who wanted to encourage her young son's progress on the piano. She brought tickets to the Paderewski performance. Ignacy Jan Paderewski was a world-class Polish pianist who toured all over America. When the night of the performance came, the eager mother and son found their seats at the very front of the concert hall. They saw the majestic Steinway stage center, almost within reach. The mother saw someone she knew and went over and started a quick chat before the performance. As she got involved in the conversation, her nine-year-old boy bounded up on the stage, sat right down at the Steinway, and started playing "chopsticks." The crowd booed. The mother was mortified.

Paderewski heard the racket behind the stage, and instead of joining the mob, he nobly walked out onto the stage, sat down beside the young boy and said, "Son, don't quit playing. Just don't quit. Just keep playing." That evening, Paderewski performed for the crowd, but this time, as a duet. He played a masterful concerto and composed it around the boy's song. It was a beautiful melody. The crowd stood to their feet and rang out in applause as both of them played together. Something that wasn't planned became a new thing that was absolutely beautiful.

If you're out in life doing your best and it sounds like "chopsticks," don't worry. The Master Musician, King Jesus, is always by your side (Hebrews 13:5). He will sit down right beside you and say, "Don't quit playing. Keep doing your best. I'm going to make this simple effort into a thing of beauty. I'm going to make you better than your wildest dreams. This is going to turn out better than you ever thought it could. Just don't quit!"

APPLICATION

What areas in your life do you need to take responsibility for? What areas do you need to remind yourself to keep going and not quit?

BE WILLING TO WORK

If you want something in life, you're going to have to work for it. You can't just dream or wish for it; you have to go out there, make a plan, work for it, and never give up. You must be willing to work for what you want. God gave Israel a supernatural victory at Jericho, but they had to get themselves to the fight. They had to get up, put on their armor, and obey the direction of the Lord. The walls of Jericho didn't fall down on their own. They fell because Israel was obedient to what God told them to do, and they went out and followed God's plan.

The land of Israel was promised to them, but they still had to go out and take it, city by city, hill by hill, valley by valley. God was on their side, but they had to fight for every inch of ground they got. If you want to receive the fullness of the provision that God has for you, it will take a holy tenacity and a never-give-up attitude.

During World War II, Winston Churchill was known as the "British Bulldog" because of his refusal to surrender the war under any circumstances. The bulldog's nose is slightly turned backwards so that it can latch on in a death-grip bite on its foe and still breath during the fight. In 1941, Churchill famously said, *"This is the lesson: never give in, never give in, never, never, never, never — in nothing, great or small, large or petty — never give in except to convictions of honor and good sense." iv* The same is true for you. If you want to overcome your problems and receive the provision of God, don't be surprised if you find yourself in a dogfight.

You have a Heavenly assignment, and you have a call from God on your life. But if you received the fullness of your provision too early, it would destroy you. Proverbs 20:21 says, *"An inheritance claimed too soon will not be blessed at the end"* (NIV). Wealth without work will not last. God provides worms for birds, but He doesn't present the worms on a platter every morning at 7:00 am. They have to get up, leave the nest, and go find them. It's still true that the early bird gets the worm.

Work is a gift from God. Ecclesiastes 5:18–20 (NKJV) says, *"It is good and fitting for one to eat and drink, and to enjoy the good of all his labor in which he toils under the sun all the days of his life which God gives him; for it is his heritage. As for every man to whom God has given riches and wealth, and given him power to eat of it, to receive his heritage and rejoice in his labor—this is the gift of God. For he will not dwell unduly on the days of his life, because God keeps him busy with the joy of his heart."*

You need to get excited about your job and start seeing it as a gift from God. How you view your work can affect you a great deal. The same job from a different perspective can change your life. The story is told of a stranger who came to three workmen, all of whom were employed to do the same job. He stopped and asked the workers what they were doing. The first man growled, "I'm breaking rocks." The second man snarled and said, "I'm making a living." The third man said, with a smile, "I am building a cathedral."

APPLICATION

How do you see your job? Are you breaking rocks or building a cathedral? Take some time to read Ecclesiastes 5:18–20. What is the Lord telling you about your job?

DAY 20
LET IT GO

If you want to move forward in life, you've got to spend more time looking out of the windshield than you do in the rear-view mirror. There is nothing you can do about anything that happened in your past. The past is done. Those days are over. All that you have is today and the days ahead of you. You've got to let the past go. Don't waste time thinking about what could've been, might've been, or should've been. If you spend all of your energy fighting for what you cannot change, you won't have any strength for the battles of the day.

Let the past go. Stop fighting for what you cannot change. Do you know why Israel didn't go back to Egypt? It wasn't because they were dedicated to God or believed in Moses. They didn't go back to Egypt because the Red Sea closed. They couldn't swim that far. They had to move forward because it was their only option.

There are some things in life that cannot be changed, no matter what you say, what you do, or how badly you wish things were different. You've just got to leave them in the past and look forward to the future. Did you experience hardship, heartache, or hazard? Whatever happened, it's time to close that chapter in your mind, get over it once and for all, and look to your future in Jesus.

Hardships and difficulties are a normal part of the Christian life. Remember, Joseph was sold into slavery, David had to run for his life, Paul was imprisoned, and Jesus was betrayed and died on Calvary. It's time to move on from the past. Today is the day when you can take those memories, those dreams, and those relationships, and finally and fully lay them down at the foot of the Cross.

You can reach for greatness. You can go through the problem. You are enough. It's not what you're going *through*, it's what you're going *to* that makes the difference. Reach out for what God has for you tomorrow. Your future is where you're going. Let the past be done now, because if you always live in the past, it will destroy your future.

God has good plans in store for your life. His plans are to prosper you and not to harm you, to give you a hope and future. Romans 8:28 says, *"We know that in all things God works for the good of those who love him, who have been called according to his purpose"* (NIV). God can cause all things to work for your good. He can cause a broken past to turn into an incredible future.

Your past does not define you. The Word of God is what defines you. If you want to know who you are, stop looking to the world, to your friends, or to your past. Look to the Bible and you will find that your identity is in Christ.

APPLICATION

Take some time and lay everything out before God that you need to give to Him. Write it all down. All of it. When it's all out on the table, submit it back to Him. Give God your past, your present, your future. Give Him your hopes and dreams. Open every corner of your heart to His light and healing. And then, open your Bible and discover who you really are.

ADMIT WHEN YOU'RE WRONG

A critical step to getting out of any problem as fast as possible — when you're the one at fault — is admitting when you make a mistake. When you're in the wrong, don't ignore it and don't blame someone else. If it was your error, admit it and move on. Not taking responsibility for your own faults will only hurt you and send you for another lap or so around the mountain in the wilderness.

Admission of fault is a rare trait in the world, but it is an honorable one. It is also good for your heart and soul. In Psalm 32:5, when David prayed to the Lord about his own sins and iniquities, he found forgiveness: *"Then I acknowledged my sin to you and did not cover up my iniquity. I said, 'I will confess my transgressions to the* LORD.*' And you forgave the guilt of my sin"* (NIV). It was when David was honest before the Lord that he was restored.

In the New Testament, James also wrote about it. He exhorted the early church that the benefits of confession would open the door for sought-after healing. He wrote, *"Confess your sins to each other and pray for each other so that you may be healed. The prayer of a righteous person is powerful and effective"* (James 5:16, NIV). Whether it's wrongdoing, sin, or a mistake, it is when you admit your faults that you expedite the process of finding the freedom you seek.

Assigning blame to other people won't get you anywhere in life. We've been blaming our mistakes on others ever since Adam and Eve ate the forbidden fruit. We've got to stop playing the blame game. If you're wrong, admit it. No good will come into your life if you constantly see yourself as an eternal victim. Life is too short to tether your emotions to something that happened 10 years ago.

It's about ownership. You've got to take charge of your life or someone else will. You've got to plan out your life, or life will happen to you. What do you want to see happen in your future? Do you want to achieve a dream, find success, or enjoy life-giving relationships? One of the first steps to reaching any goal is to be honest with yourself about where you are right now.

If you were in the wrong about something, own your mistake and admit your fault. Admit it, receive forgiveness, let the past go, and face forward. Now you're set up to move forward. If you assume responsibility for the consequences that you are responsible for, you'll accelerate your time out of the wilderness and position yourself for the next step towards the promised land.

APPLICATION

What areas in your life do you need to take ownership of? Is there someone you need to reconcile with, ask for forgiveness, or admit you were wrong about something? Spend some time in prayer, and honestly ask the Lord what your part may be in this step.

FORGIVE, FORGIVE, FORGIVE

Forgiveness is one of the most important characteristics in any Believer's life. Forgiveness and love are like twins. It's hard to have one without the other. If you have a heart of love, you will be able to forgive, and if you forgive, your heart gains the capacity to love again. Both gifts are offered to us from our Heavenly Father — abundant forgiveness and endless love.

We all have opportunities to extend love and forgiveness as we go through troubles, conflicts, and problems in life. In John 16:33, Jesus told us that we would have trouble in the world. But the key for the Believer, and the key to how quickly we go through problems has always been gauged by how we respond in those problems. Forgiveness is the master key that liberates you from your own emotional prison, where you are the only prisoner, and the person you won't forgive is on the other side of the door.

When you extend forgiveness, you will find benefits that help you in life. As Jesus was preaching the Sermon on the Mount in Matthew 5–7, He gave us what is known as the Lord's Prayer. In Matthew 6:12, He exhorted us to forgive others as we ourselves have been forgiven. Forgiveness is not optional. If you want to remove every obstacle you can that would keep you in the problem, forgive as many people as you can. But you will extend your time in the problem by nursing a grudge and refusing forgiveness. If you do not forgive somebody else, God cannot forgive you. Verses 14–15 of Matthew say, *"For if you forgive other people when they sin against you, your heavenly Father will also forgive you. But if you do not forgive others their sins, your Father will not forgive your sins"* (NIV). Is there someone in your past that you cannot forgive? You need to forgive them today, instantly. Not for their benefit, but for yours. Forgiveness is the key that unlocks the handcuffs of hatred.

There was once a young man who committed a crime. In the courtroom, he was sentenced to 10 years in prison, handcuffed, and led out. As he was walking by, his father said, "Don't ever think about coming home again. You've ruined our name." When the time came for his release from prison, he wrote a letter to his father asking if he would forgive him. He wrote, *I'm going to ride the train that comes by the ranch. If you will forgive me, please tie a white cloth in the tree by the track. But if there's no white cloth in that tree, I'll keep going and will never try to contact you again.* The day came for his release. He went to the train. He got on, and with every turn of the wheel, the anxiety grew and his heartbeat raced faster. The train was passing through the family ranch, and he couldn't bring himself to see if that white cloth was in the tree. So, he asked the passenger beside him, "Would you look out the window and see if there is a white cloth in the tree?" The passenger stuck his head out the window and said, "No, there's not one white cloth in that tree, there are hundreds of white cloths in that tree. There are white cloths on the clothesline. There are white cloths on every bush on that ranch. What does it mean?" He jumped off the train and said, "It means I'm forgiven by my father, and I'm going home!"

APPLICATION

You have the same forgiveness abundantly offered to you today from your Heavenly Father. Romans 5:8 says, *"But God demonstrates his own love for us in this: While we were still sinners, Christ died for us"* (NIV). His arms are extended to you. You can find full forgiveness, mercy, and redemption in this great God who loves you. Jesus already paid the price at the Cross. In Him, your Father in Heaven has forgiven you. Spend time in prayer today. Receive the forgiveness of the Lord. Know that because of Jesus, right now, you are justified, redeemed, and set free. Receive the full benefits of forgiveness from the Lord today.

DAY 23

THE POWER OF GENEROSITY

There is a Biblical principle that will unlock abundant provision, peace, and joy in your life. It is contrary to the ways of the world, but perfectly in line with the laws of the Kingdom of God. If you can learn to harness the power of generosity, sowing and reaping, and let your life become a river to others, you will shorten your time in the problem.

Hearts that are hard towards the needs of others are hearts that cannot easily receive very much from God. But those who are generous to those in need, will find assistance from Heaven and grace for the times when they themselves are in need.

In Luke 6:38, Jesus said, *"Give, and it will be given to you: good measure, pressed down, shaken together, and running over will be put into your bosom. For with the same measure that you use, it will be measured back to you"* (NKJV). It is when our hands are open to others and open to God, that we find He will keep supplying us with everything that we need.

There is a law in the Bible, and it is that givers gain and that everything that God controls, gives. God is the greatest giver of all. God made a plan for man's salvation and gave His only begotten Son to save the world. Jesus came to seek and save the lost, and He gave up His life on Calvary's tree. The Holy Spirit gave power to the 120 Believers in the upper room in Jerusalem on the day of Pentecost.

Giving is about the heart more than the gift. In Luke 21, when the widow gave her offering to the temple, Jesus said, *"Truly I say to you that this poor widow has put in more than all; for all these out of their abundance have put in offerings for God, but she out of her poverty put in all the livelihood that she had"* (v. 3–4, NKJV). Giving untethers your heart from the things of the world and reconnects you to the Kingdom of God.

In Matthew 6:22–23, Jesus said, *"The lamp of the body is the eye. If therefore your eye is good, your whole body will be full of light. But if your eye is bad, your whole body will be full of darkness. If therefore the light that is in you is darkness, how great is that darkness!"* (NKJV). An idiom is a saying, such as, "it's raining cats and dogs," to mean that it is raining a lot. Or "he's sawing logs," which means someone is asleep. It is a saying that has a meaning behind it. In Hebrew, a "good eye" was an idiom for generosity and how generosity brings light to the heart and soul. [v]

When you have a heart that gives, you have proof that the cancer of greed has not consumed your soul. How you treat someone else in their day of trouble is going to determine how God is going to treat you in your day of trouble. Isaiah wrote about how God will help those who make it a practice to give to others and reach out to those in need. *"If you extend your soul to the hungry and satisfy the afflicted soul, then your light shall dawn in the darkness, and your darkness shall be as the noonday. The LORD will guide you continually, and satisfy your soul in drought, and strengthen your bones; you shall be like a watered garden, and like a spring of water, whose waters do not fail"* (Isaiah 58:10–11, NKJV).

APPLICATION

We make a living by what we get out of life, but we make a life by what we give. What are you giving? What do you need to give?

REFUSE SELF-PITY

Self-pity is an invisible chain that will do nothing but take more from your life. Self-pity will never get you anywhere, will never give you anything, and will continue to take all it can from you for as long as you allow it to. Refuse to indulge in self-pity when life hands you a raw deal.

Accept the fact that nobody gets through life without some sorrow or misfortune. Self-pity is a sin. Why? Because it obliterates all hope and trust in God and puts oneself on the throne. If your thoughts are consumed with self-centeredness, you will live a myopic life where everything is about you.

It does you no good at all to mope or cry and say, "No one loves me. I think I'll go out in the garden and eat worms." You can do that if you want, and you can suck your thumb until it falls off, but nobody will care, and it will benefit you nothing. Have you been knocked down flat on your face? Get up and dust yourself off. You've got to remember who you are, whose you are, and where you're going. The Bible says that you're a child of the King and that you have the royal blood of Heaven flowing through your veins. You've got to lift your eyes off of the here and now and look to Jesus, the Author and Perfector of your faith. You've got to fill your mind with the Word of God. The Bible says, *"out of the abundance of the heart his mouth speaks"* (Luke 6:45, NKJV). What do you want to fill your heart with?

You can focus on your problems, or you can lift your eyes to the hills, where your help comes from. You've got to remember that *"greater is he that is in you, than he that is in the world"* (1 John 4:4, KJV). You've got to act like it, think like it, and talk like it. You've got to remember that you're a child of the King. If you fill your mind and heart with the

Word of God, nothing will be impossible for you. There's a right way and a wrong way to react when problems come your way. Here's the right way: Say, "Glory to God, I got fired. How can I get a better job unless I lose this one? I know that God will supply all my needs according to His riches and glory." When your heart is full of faith, when you refuse self-pity, and when your gaze is ever towards Heaven for your redemption and supply, you will move yourself out of the problem, and set yourself up for the promised provision.

When you react the right way to problems and have a heart that is fully given over to the Lord, don't be surprised if God looks down from Heaven and says, "Now look at that heart. Do you hear all that praise? He's learned the principle. He's refusing self-pity and he is looking to Me for all his needs. Now then, let's open the floodgates of blessing for him. Let's make the crooked way straight. Let's make a way where there seems to be no way. Let's bring him into his inheritance and fill his cup to overflowing, conquer his enemies, and silence his accusers. I will give him houses he didn't build and wells he didn't dig. I will bless him with vineyards he didn't plant and shower him with showers of blessing."

In 1 Samuel 30, David and all of his men returned to Ziklag only to find the city burned and all of their wives and children taken captive by the Amalekites. But David *"strengthened himself in the Lord his God"* (v. 6, NKJV). When you get your focus off of yourself and onto God, you expedite the timeline for getting yourself out of your current problem.

APPLICATION

Fill your heart with praise and look to God for all your needs. Refuse self-pity and strengthen yourself in the Lord. What problems can you submit to the Lord today, never to think about them again?

DAY 25
LISTEN

Another step in shortening your stay in the wilderness is to listen, really listen. This means giving people your undivided attention, putting aside your feelings, and trying to understand their point of view when they are talking to you. If you've been married for any length of time, you and your spouse have had what I call an "intensive conversation" from time to time. When your spouse is talking, you've got to learn to listen to what they're saying. Listening is not ignoring what they're saying and rehearsing what you're going to say as soon as they take a breath.

You must learn to listen to the people in your life and also learn to listen to God. Ecclesiastes 5:2 says, *"Do not be quick with your mouth, do not be hasty in your heart to utter anything before God. God is in heaven and you are on earth, so let your words be few"* (NIV). Learning to listen is a powerful spiritual principle.

When Samuel was just a boy and growing up under Eli's tutelage, God woke him up in the night to speak to him. When Samuel thought it was Eli calling, Eli said to Samuel, *"Go, lie down; and it shall be, if He calls you, that you must say, 'Speak, LORD, for Your servant hears'"* (1 Samuel 3:9, NKJV).

Pew Research released a study that found one third of children in the U.S. are living with an unmarried parent,[vi] which means they are lacking consistent time with either their mother or father. Additionally, most American children spend up to five hours a day in front of a screen.[vii] Who do you think has the most influence on your children? As the spiritual leader of your house, it's your job to be the primary influence in the lives of your children. It is both your voice and your ear that they need access to as they navigate the perils of life.

You also must learn to control your tongue. Proverbs 13:3 says, *"He who guards his mouth preserves his life"* (NKJV). You may not want to control your tongue, but you can control your tongue. The Bible says that when you stand before God, you're going to give an account for every word, every thought, and every deed of your life (Matthew 12:36–37; Romans 14:12).

You will be justified or condemned by the words that you speak. It will be one or the other, with nothing in between. You must be careful of what you say because you're going to hear it again. If you love life and want to see good days, refrain your tongue from evil and keep your lips from speaking deceit (1 Peter 3:10).

Be careful about the words that you use about other people. When you're talking about other people, you're talking about God's children. You may not like them, but you need to remember that God loves them as much as He loves you.

If you choose to speak, choose wisely. You don't have to say the first thing that comes to your mind. And you don't have to respond immediately. You can think about your words, choose your words, and you can choose your tone of voice when you speak.

APPLICATION

Look up some Scriptures in the Bible about guarding your tongue. What stands out to you? Who in your life comes to mind as someone that you need to listen to more?

DAY 26

THE PEACEMAKER

Another way to shorten your stay in the problem is to purpose in your heart to be a peacemaker. Jesus said, *"Blessed are the peacemakers, for they will be called children of God"* (Matthew 5:9, NIV). Those who are called "children of God" are peacemakers. They are not those who go around stirring up gossip, causing strife, or dividing friendships.

Peacemakers mend the quarrel. Peacemakers respond to anger with a gentle tongue (Proverbs 15:1). The Bible says it this way: *"'Be angry, and do not sin': do not let the sun go down on your wrath, nor give place to the devil"* (Ephesians 4:26–27, NKJV). It's important that you do whatever you need to do to not let the day end while you are still burning up with anger. Have you ever gone to bed mad as a hornet? Are you angry with someone right now? Now is the time and today is the day to pursue peace and be reconciled.

Jesus specifically addressed how we should deal with anger in Matthew 5:21–26. In the middle of the discourse, he says, *"if you bring your gift to the altar, and there remember that your brother has something against you, leave your gift there before the altar, and go your way. First be reconciled to your brother, and then come and offer your gift"* (v. 23–24, NKJV). You will enjoy a blessed life and an expedited exit from your current problems if you can live in peace with your friends, family, and your acquaintances.

Reconciliation will open more doors for you that will lead you out of the wilderness that you didn't even know were available to you. David wrote, *"Behold, how good and how pleasant it is for brethren to dwell together in unity!"* (Psalm 133:1, NKJV). When you are "dwelling together in unity" with the people in your life, you will enjoy the blessings of reconciliation and fellowship that will strengthen your heart and help you move towards your provision.

When my father was alive, one day I asked him about Deuteronomy 6:6. The text says, *"These commandments that I give you today are to be on your hearts"* (NIV). I quizzed him about why the Bible says the words would be on the heart. Why didn't God say that He would place the words in our hearts? There's a lot of difference between on and in. My father's response was, "It's not within the preacher's power to place divine teaching directly in the heart. All he can do is place the Word of God on the surface of the heart so that when the heart breaks, it opens, and the Word of God drops in as a precious seed. It is then rooted in the soil of the soul." You have the choice to let the Word of God come into your heart, take deep root, and bring supernatural change to your life.

It's up to you. You can take control of your thoughts, your words, and your life. If you don't, someone else will. In James 3:1–11, he compares the tongue to a bit in a horse's mouth, a rudder that guides a ship, and a spark that can cause a forest fire. Your tongue directs your life, and the words you say can either bring division or peace, rivalry or reconciliation.

APPLICATION

Spend some time in prayer today. Commit your tongue and the words you speak to the Lord. Like Isaiah, let the burning coal of cleansing touch your lips. Ask the Lord for a mouth that only speaks righteousness and words that bring peace. (Proverbs 21:23; Matthew 15:11; Ephesians 4:29; Colossians 4:6)

PART THREE

PROVISION

DAY 27

DESTINED
FOR DIADEMS

The story is told of a Native American who found an eagle's egg and put it in the nest of a prairie chicken. When the eaglet hatched, it was born into a brood of prairie chickens and grew up with them. All his life, the eagle, thinking that he was a prairie chicken, did exactly what the other prairie chickens did. He scratched in the dirt for seeds and worms. He cackled and he clucked. He scurried away from would-be predators. He dared not fly, and when he did, it was only a few feet off the ground because that's as far as everybody else around him could fly.

Years passed, and the eaglet grew into a strong and powerful eagle. One day, he looked up and saw a magnificent bird far above him in the cloudless sky, flying with majestic grace on the powerful wind currents. It soared across the sky, scarcely beating its powerful wings. The eagle looked at the other prairie chickens and said, "What a beautiful and majestic bird that is. What kind of bird is that?" One of the prairie chickens looked at the eagle and said, "That is the mighty eagle, the chief of all birds." The prairie chicken paused to peck and scratch in the dirt and then continued, "But don't even dare think that you can fly like that eagle. You can never be what that eagle is. You are nothing more than a common prairie chicken." And though his heart leapt within him, the earth-bound eagle, so deceived, pushed his hopes aside, never gave it another thought, and died thinking he was a prairie chicken.

What the eagle believed about himself completely controlled his potential and his accomplishments. God designed him to soar in the sky. He was engineered by the divine Architect of the ages for high adventure, yet he pecked for worms and scratched for bugs in the dirt, cackling and clucking because he believed that was all he was good for and as high as he could achieve.

PROVISION

You will do the same if you do not see yourself as God sees you. Stop seeing yourself like other people may see you. Stop believing ideas or words that other people have said about you. Start seeing yourself as God sees you. You are a divine creature, and you have a divine purpose locked within you that no one else on this earth can match. You've got to lay aside your past, forget about your mistakes (Philippians 3:12–14), and look for the opportunities that God has given you to reach your divine destiny.

Maybe you have a book to write. Maybe you have a song to sing. Maybe you have a child to raise who can spiritually change the destiny of the nation. Some of you have a gift inside of you just looking for a place to explode. The royal blood of Heaven is flowing in your veins. You are a co-heir with Jesus Christ (Romans 8:17) in a Kingdom that shall never end. You've got to believe that God does not manufacture junk and that He does not sponsor flops. Your future is far greater than anything that you can possibly imagine. Because of what Jesus accomplished on the Cross, you are destined for high flight. When you see yourself as God sees you, you will never be satisfied with merely scratching around with prairie chickens. Start looking for high flight on the wings of faith that helps you accomplish the impossible, because nothing is impossible to those that believe and are called according to the purposes of God.

APPLICATION

Write down what it means to you to "shake off a prairie chicken attitude." It's time for you to look up and swing for the fences. It's time for you to spread your wings and fly. It's time for you to believe that you are destined for diadems.

DAY 28

ATTACKING FEAR

If you want to inherit the provision that God has for you, it is absolutely essential that you learn to attack fear and never give into its debilitating distress. When Moses led Israel out of Egypt, he attacked the three problems of fear that Israel had to conquer before they could experience success.

When Israel was camped on the shores of the Red Sea, they looked up and saw Pharaoh and 600 chosen chariots of war and the world's mightiest army thundering across the desert toward them. Exodus 14:10 reads, "*...the Egyptians* *marched after them; and they were sore afraid: and the children of Israel cried out unto the LORD"* (KJV).

They were "sore afraid." It means they were terrified. In your life, when you look up and see trials and problems thundering towards you, it is easy to give into fear. It could be a medical report, a financial report, or the grades on a report card. When the fear comes, you can't give into it. You've got to stand firm in the strength of the Lord.

Do not fear death. David said: *"Yea, though I walk through the valley of the shadow of death, I will fear no evil; for You are with me; Your rod and Your staff, they comfort me"* (Psalm 23:4, NKJV). Death is a shadow, and the shadow of a lion cannot bite you. The shadow of a sword cannot cut you. The shadow of a serpent cannot harm you. Remember that Jesus Christ has so defeated death that it is nothing now but a harmless shadow. And when you walk through it, it will not hurt you or harm you because Jesus has already conquered death, hell, and the grave.

Do not fear disease. The Bible says, *"for I am the LORD, who heals you"* (Exodus 15:26, NIV). Healing of the body, mind, and soul is a benefit available to you as a Believer living in the Kingdom of God. James 5:14–16 says, *"Is anyone among you sick? Let them call the elders of the church to pray over them and anoint them with oil in the name of the Lord. And the prayer offered in faith will make the sick person well; the Lord will raise them up. If they have sinned, they will be forgiven. Therefore confess your sins to each other and pray for each other so that you may be healed. The prayer of a righteous person is powerful and effective"* (NIV). Healing is a promise from God.

Do not fear the past. The past is now behind you. Past mistakes are now buried in the deepest sea, never to be remembered again. In Jeremiah 31:34, God said, *"For I will forgive their iniquity, and their sin I will remember no more"* (NKJV).

Do not fear the future. I don't know what tomorrow holds, but I do know Who holds tomorrow. No matter what may come in the days ahead, Jesus Christ, the King of Kings and Lord of Lords, is right now, high and lifted up. He is enthroned in Heaven. He knows the end from the beginning, and He holds you in the palm of His hand. As for you, say of the Lord, *"He is my refuge and my fortress, my God, in whom I trust"* (Psalm 91:2, NIV).

APPLICATION

Spend some time meditating on Psalm 91. Write some of the verses down and pray some of the verses out loud. Which verses are you most drawn to? Who could you encourage today with a verse from Psalm 91?

FACING BITTERNESS

If you are breathing air, at one point or another, you will come face-to-face with the sting of bitter experiences, bitter conversations, or bitter encounters. Israel had to face bitterness at the waters of Marah, only three days after they had crossed the Red Sea.

You may have been raised in a church that taught that if you really live a spiritual life, you'll never have a bitter experience. I'm here to tell you that's absolutely false doctrine. Why? Because of logic. Remember Who led the children of Israel to Marah. God took them straight from the victory at the Red Sea to that bitter mudhole to show them what was in them, to test their hearts, to grow and mature them.

If you're in a Marah situation right now, there is a solution for you. You, and you alone, are the one who is in control of your thoughts, words, and prayers that can get yourself out of that bitter place as quickly as possible. The first thing you have to do is quit complaining to others and start talking to God.

You've got to open the communication lines with God and commit yourself to hours of prayer. Prayer changes things. If you're standing by a bitter pool, lift your voice to Heaven. God does not enter the equation until you've spent time in prayer over the situation. And if God is removed from the equation, you could live there the rest of your life. At Marah, Moses prayed. When Moses prayed, God showed him the solution. Solutions come down when prayers go up.

The solution in Exodus 15:22–27 is that God showed Moses a tree. Moses cut the tree down and threw it into the bitter pool, and the water became fit to drink. It was

PROVISION

a supernatural miracle. The application in this story is also the application to your bitterness.

Jesus Christ was taken to Calvary and nailed to the cursed tree. And when that cursed tree, the Cross, is applied and plunges into the bitter pool of your soul, supernaturally and instantaneously, the bitterness of your life will disappear. The bitterness of your marriage will disappear. The bitterness of your memories will disappear. Life instantly, suddenly, miraculously becomes sweet and joyous and full of peace, a peace that surpasses understanding.

A woman named Helen Howarth Lemmel wrote the hymn "Turn Your Eyes Upon Jesus." [viii] The chorus reads, *"Turn your eyes upon Jesus, look full in His wonderful face, and the things of earth will grow strangely dim, in the light of His glory and grace."* If you're in a bitter situation, a bitter relationship, or have bitter corners in your heart, you can choose today to turn your eyes upon Jesus. Cast your cares upon the Lord today, for He cares for you. In 1678, John Bunyan wrote *The Pilgrim's Progress*. It is an allegory about a man named Christian on his way to the Celestial City. When Christian arrives at the Cross, the burden on his back is loosed from his shoulders, falls off his back, and is seen no more. [ix]

APPLICATION

Today, you can do the same. You can come boldly to the throne of grace and lay your burdens down at the foot of the Cross. God is a Great Redeemer. In Him, you can exchange bitterness for joy, ashes for beauty, and death for life. What do you need to lay down at the foot of the Cross today?

PROVISION

THE POWER OF SELF-CONTROL

As Christians, we are to be self-controlled in every area of our lives. You have the ability to control your thoughts, and your thoughts control so much of your life, which will affect your mood, your words, your relationships, and your destiny. You are in control of yourself. Not someone else, not your environment, not the people around you, but you.

You control what you do with your free time in the evening. If you spend your evenings watching TV or scrolling endlessly online, you're wasting your time and could be foregoing your call from God. The late Dr. David Wilkerson wrote his story in *The Cross and Switchblade*. He sold his TV to spend time in prayer, and his prayer life is what led him to his place in ministry, eventually founding Times Square Church and Teen Challenge. [x]

Proverbs 16:32 says, *"He who rules his spirit* [is better] *than he who takes a city"* (NKJV). If you can control yourself, then you can overcome anything, no matter what circumstances are around you. During the Holocaust, a Jewish doctor named Dr. Viktor Frankl was captured by the Nazis. They killed his family, tattooed his arm, gave him another name, and shaved his head. Sitting in the darkness of his cell, he said that he made up his mind that regardless of how difficult the environment was, regardless of how difficult the conditions were, and regardless of how difficult this thing was that they were putting him through, these Nazis could not control the thoughts he decided to think about in his own private time. And so, in the theater of his mind, he lived in paradise while living in hell. [xi]

Controlling your thoughts is the key to controlling your life, which will lead you to your destiny. As Proverbs 23:7 says, *"as he thinketh in his heart, so is he"* (KJV). Self-control is one of the Bible's most valuable lessons. It is the ability to make yourself do the things you have to when you don't want to and do them with excellence. Life is not about doing what you want; it's about doing what you must do. That's self-control.

Without self-control, your life is already over. You may be wealthy, but without self-control, poverty is on the way. You may be powerful, but without self-control, your power and influence will not last. In the battle for self-control, the enemy is you. The war of the soul is a civil war on the inside. It is the desires of the flesh raging against the call of the spirit. You must put off the old man, renew your mind by the Word, and commit daily to full allegiance to Jesus Christ.

Romans 12:2 says, *"Do not be conformed to this world, but be transformed by the renewing of your mind, that you may prove what is that good and acceptable and perfect will of God"* (NKJV). You and you alone, control the gate of your mind. You can choose to fill your mind with the things of the world, or you can meditate on the things of God. *"Whatever things are true, whatever things are noble, whatever things are just, whatever things are pure, whatever things are lovely, whatever things are of good report, if there is any virtue and if there is anything praiseworthy—meditate on these things"* (Philippians 4:8, NKJV).

APPLICATION

Your doubts are the traitors to your dreams. Your fears strangle your hopes and keep you from climbing the stairway to the stars. Your habits are born of your free will, and they will lead you into captivity or into paradise. What is the Lord telling you to do regarding self-control, your time, and the thoughts you fill your mind with?

DAY 31

THREE PORTRAITS

Moses was a poet, a prophet, and a lawgiver. His leadership crushed mighty Egypt and the majesty of Pharaoh's government. Yet for Moses to fulfill the call of God on his life, he had to overcome one of the major hurdles of life: self-control.

Moses lost his temper three times in life, and each one cost him dearly. The first time he lost his temper, he murdered an Egyptian. That sent him to the back side of the wilderness for 40 years. The second time was when he came down from Mount Sinai carrying the Ten

Commandments. When he saw Israel worshiping an idol, he smashed the tablets down and had to return to the mountain once more. The third time he lost his temper, God told Moses to speak to a rock for water to pour out. Yet instead of speaking to it, in anger, he smote the rock (Numbers 20:8–12).

The consequences of losing his temper, hence his self-control, were severe. God did not allow Moses to enter into the Promised Land. God said to Moses, *"Because you did not trust in me enough to honor me as holy in the sight of the Israelites, you will not bring this community into the land I give them"* (v. 12, NIV). Entering the Promised Land was his life-long dream, but he would never see it. Take note, because a temper that is left unchecked and out of control will keep you from realizing your dreams.

David, the Psalmist and King of Israel, also had to learn the consequences of a lack of self-control. He is the man whom the Bible calls a man after God's own heart (Acts 13:22), the one who would not touch Saul when he was in his hand (1 Samuel 24), and the one who struck down mighty Goliath in the Valley of Elah (1 Samuel 17). And yet, one spring, when kings go off to war, David sent Joab out with the army, but David stayed behind. One night,

PROVISION

he saw Bathsheba, which led to her pregnancy and the plot to kill Uriah. For his lack of self-control, God sent the prophet Nathan to inform David what his punishment would be (2 Samuel 12).

Conversely, Jesus Christ was the ultimate picture of self-control. From His prayer of anguish in the Garden of Gethsemane, to the flogging and mocking at the hands of the Praetorian Guard, to carrying the Cross along the Via Dolorosa, and finally to Calvary's hill, Jesus Christ, the Lamb of God, never once faltered.

Put in your mind this fact: that this Rabbi, Jesus of Nazareth, had all power in Heaven and on earth. He was and is the Son of God, the *"Alpha and the Omega, Beginning and the End, the First and the Last"* (Revelation 22:13, NKJV). He is the One who, at any moment, could have called on His Father and at once been given more than 12 legions of angels (Matthew 26:53).

Jesus had all power in Heaven and on earth, and yet out of love and obedience, He willingly gave Himself as the propitiation of sin and became the Savior of the world. Jesus was the ultimate picture of self-control. Even on the Cross, even bloodied and bruised, He prayed,

"Father, forgive them; for they know not what they do" (Luke 23:34, KJV).

APPLICATION

Self-control is one of the absolute essentials to getting out of your problem. The presence or lack of self-control in your life will determine your future. In what areas of your life do you need more self-control?

WISDOM AND WEALTH

Wisdom and wealth are inseparable partners. Proverbs 8:18–19 says of wisdom, *"Riches and honor are with me, enduring riches and righteousness. My fruit is better than gold, yes, than fine gold, and my revenue than choice silver"* (NKJV). On the one hand, wisdom will bring riches, but on the other hand, a person who inherits a fortune and does not have the wisdom to manage it will ultimately lose it.

It has often been said that a fool and his money are soon parted. Put another way, genius has limits; foolishness does not. There's a great difference between knowledge and wisdom. Knowledge is the retention of facts. Wisdom is knowing how to manage those facts. You may know a lot of facts, but if you can't put them all together to make an intelligent decision, facts alone won't help you get to where you're trying to go.

When the Titanic was sinking in the frigid waters of the Atlantic, a frightened woman found her place in a lifeboat that was about to be lowered into the freezing waters. She suddenly thought of something she needed and asked permission to return to her stateroom before the boat was lowered. She was granted three minutes, or they would lower the boat and leave her on the sinking ship.

She ran across the deck that was already tilting, raced through the gambling room and the piles of money, and, with all her might, sprinted to her stateroom. She pushed aside her former treasured jewelry and, above her bed, found her prize: three oranges. Just a few hours earlier, she never would have chosen three measly oranges over money, jewels, and clothes, but everything had changed and the common was now priceless. Not knowing how long she would be at sea, wisdom chose common fruit over rubies, diamonds, silver, and gold.

Right now, whether you comprehend it or not, you are making choices that will affect the outcome of your life forever. Make no mistake, in a figurative sense, you're on the Titanic. The Bible says, *"Heaven and earth will pass away"* (Matthew 24:35, NKJV). John the Baptist said of Jesus that *"His winnowing fork is in his hand, and he will clear his threshing floor, gathering his wheat into the barn and burning up the chaff"* (Matthew 3:12, NIV). And Jesus Himself said, *"Behold, I am coming quickly, and My reward is with Me, to give to every one according to his work"* (Revelation 22:12, NKJV).

With wisdom, you can make decisions about your life that will bring rewards into your future. Proverbs 3:13–16 says, *"Happy is the man who finds wisdom, and the man who gains understanding; for her proceeds are better than the profits of silver, and her gain than fine gold. She is more precious than rubies, and all the things you may desire cannot compare with her. Length of days is in her right hand, in her left hand riches and honor"* (NKJV). You must find wisdom quickly, because very soon, priceless things will become worthless, and worthless things will become priceless.

You are one breath away from eternity. The decisions you make affect the rest of your life and follow you into eternity. Now is not the time to straddle the fence of life with one foot in the church and one foot in the world. If you would follow wisdom's advice, you must make it your primary mission in life to live fully, wholeheartedly, and unequivocally for Jesus.

APPLICATION

What changes do you need to make to bring wisdom into every area of your life?

THE CUSP OF GREATNESS

God had given the promise of entering the land of Canaan, the land of Israel, to Abraham, Isaac, and Jacob. They had cherished the promise, believed in the promise, and quoted it for centuries. From one generation to the next, they had passed down the promise of God, believing that one day, God would come through.

It is an incredible story, and it holds a great lesson for us. Because when the people of Israel finally got to the very borders of the Promised Land, a day that their ancestors had dreamed about, told stories about, and prayed for, they failed. They lost their opportunity.

When they were within eyesight of the long-awaited promise, they rejected it. Because of fear, lack of faith, and the inability to comprehend the divine wisdom to walk into the wealth that God had prepared for them for centuries, they made an irreversible mistake. And they died in the wilderness because they lacked the insight and understanding to grasp how priceless are the promises of God.

They accepted the opinion of 10 men, a small committee of chosen leaders. Those 10 spies came back and said that they couldn't take the land in spite of all the miracles God had been doing in front of their eyes since they left Egypt. On the very cusp of the greatest moment of their lives, they gave into a negative "we-can't-do-it" mindset. They stumbled at the threshold of their destiny and did not take one step into the Promised Land that was directly within reach.

Because they accepted the opinions of men over the Word and promises of God, they died in the wilderness. Take heed of their story because the same thing can happen to you unless you have the wisdom and courage to walk in the wealth that God has promised you through His Word. On the greatest day of your life, don't give into fear. You have to be able to comprehend the day of your destiny. For when it comes, you must strike opportunity with the anvil of faith in God and hope in His Word, or you too, may never enter in.

Don't die in the wilderness of unbelief. Don't give up on the verge of faith. Dare to believe that God has better plans for your life than you could possibly imagine. Yield to the hope that He really is that good, really does love you that much, and that with Him, you really can inherit the provision He has for you. You have to believe. You have to rise up in faith. You have to take the step out of the camp in the wilderness, set your face like flint towards the promised land, and move forward into His good plans for you.

Believe He is ever with you. Believe He is Jehovah Shammah, the God who is there. Believe His Word in which He has said, *"Never will I leave you; never will I forsake you"* (Hebrews 13:5, NIV). He's with you in the fiery furnace and He's with you in the lion's den. He's with you at Marah and He's with you in the valley of the shadow of death. He's with you in the hour of sickness and He's with you in financial crisis. No matter what, hold on to hope and trust that He is with you, He will not fail you, and He will never leave you.

APPLICATION

What is your promised land? Spend time in prayer asking the Lord for the wisdom to grasp your day of destiny and the faith to reach out and lay hold of it when it is within reach.

DAY 34

WISDOM SOLVES PROBLEMS

Wisdom solves problems. The problem may be in your marriage, your business, or your career, but the answer to your problem can be found through wisdom. You've got to stop ignoring the problem and solve it before the next one comes, because no one ever gets beyond the reach of a problem. Do whatever you need to do to find the wisdom you need to solve your problems.

Problems in life are inevitable. The sooner you accept that fact, the sooner you will be able to face it and come up with a solution. You need wisdom to help you solve your problems. Proverbs 4:7–9 says, *"Wisdom is the principal thing; therefore get wisdom. And in all your getting, get understanding. Exalt her, and she will promote you; she will bring you honor, when you embrace her. She will place on your head an ornament of grace; a crown of glory she will deliver to you"* (NKJV). If you can fill your life with wisdom, you will keep yourself one step ahead of getting stuck in your problems.

Wisdom solves problems. In the Northeastern United States, codfish is a big commercial business. So much so, that there was a market for codfish all over America. But the codfish business had a problem. When they shipped the fish across the country, by the time they arrived, they would no longer be in their prime. At first, the shippers tried to freeze the codfish in the Northeast before shipping them out. But that destroyed the taste of the codfish. Then they shipped the codfish alive in seawater, but that was worse. When the fish arrived at the destination, they were soft and mushy. Finally, through the wisdom of a sailor, they found the solution to the problem. The codfish were placed in a tank with their natural enemy, the catfish. From the time the codfish left the Northeast until they arrived at their destination across the nation, the ornery and aggravating catfish chased the codfish all

PROVISION

over the tank, night and day, hour after hour, right behind them. The result was that the codfish arrived at markets around the country fresh and full of flavor.

If you become complacent in your life towards your problems, sometimes God will put a catfish in your tank. He brings a problem right under your nose that you can't escape, and you can't ignore because He wants to make you stronger and draw you closer to Him. God can use problems in your life to sharpen you, to keep you alive, and to make you fresh, alert, growing, and reaching for greatness.

Wisdom is better than strength, and wisdom can deliver you from your problems. Ecclesiastes 9:14–15 says, *"There was a little city with few men in it; and a great king came against it, besieged it, and built great snares around it. Now there was found in it a poor wise man, and he by his wisdom delivered the city"* (NKJV). Wisdom delivered an entire city. Become a problem solver because your success in life will be determined by the problems you solve, or the problems you create.

APPLICATION

When problems come, find the perception of faith. When Goliath challenged all the armies of Israel to single combat, only David saw Goliath as a target too big to miss. Israel's army and David both saw the problem, but only David had a different perception. How you see the problem is the problem. Instead of focusing on the problem, find the wisdom you need to solve the problem. What problems are front of mind in your life right now? What can you do to find the wisdom you need to overcome your problems?

PROVISION

WHO YOU ARE

You need a revelation from the Word of God about who you are. When you believe what the Bible says and let its words go down into your heart, you will be forever transformed. The power of the Gospel is unto salvation, both now and forevermore. When you open your Bible, you are reading the very Word of God. You are reading words that are alive and that can bring life into your heart, spirit, and mind.

You are not who the world says you are. You are not who people may have said you are, and you are not the sum of your mistakes or shortcomings. This is who you are: you are a child of God (2 Corinthians 6:18). By the grace of God, you have been adopted as a son or daughter into the family of God. When you were adopted, your name was changed, and your future was rewritten. Now, right now, you are royalty, and the royal blood of Heaven is flowing in your veins.

You are not trapped, and you are not crushed by the power of sin. Jesus Christ defeated hell, death, and the grave. He took the keys of death and Hades, and He conquered all the power of the enemy. Jesus, the Lamb of God, the propitiation for sin, the Savior of the world, became the Mediator between man and God. At Golgotha, He freed you forever from the power of sin through the blood of the Cross.

And now you can be free forever and enjoy eternity with God. Because of what Jesus accomplished, because Jesus said, *"It is finished!"* (John 19:30, NKJV), because all of the sin of the world has already been paid, you no longer have to live under any chain or be imprisoned by any clutches of darkness. You are free. The prison door is open. The veil has been torn in two. You can cross the great divide and enter into the house of the Lord.

Not by performance, not by works, but by grace you are saved through faith in the precious blood of Jesus Christ at the Cross. And you are not only saved, but you have been equipped with everything you need to live. You have been given every good and perfect gift in the Heavenlies. You are anointed with the Holy Ghost and with fire. You have the power to tread on serpents and over scorpions. God's angels go before you, they go behind you, and they prepare a way for you.

You are not alone. Jesus has now no longer called you a servant, but a friend. And on top of that, you are an heir with Jesus Christ (Galatians 4:7). You have been endowed with every gift of a son or daughter of a King. When you got saved, you may have been poor in the eyes of the world, but when you got up from that prayer of redemption, you became an heir with He who is the Creator of the Heavens and the earth.

The Bible tells you who you are. You are an overcomer. You cannot be defeated, and you cannot be conquered (Romans 8:31–39). You have the power to walk through the valley of the shadow of death. You can walk and live in divine favor, a favor the world cannot give, and the world cannot take it away. You are blessed in your going in and you are blessed in your coming out. You are the head and not the tail, and you have been made a king and a priest unto God (Revelation 1:6). That's who you are.

APPLICATION

Open your Bible and find Scriptures that tell you who you are. Write them down, pray about them, and believe that they are true. Let the Word of God become the primary source you go to, to find your identity in Christ and as a son or daughter of the King.

DAY 36

RESPONSIBLE, ACCOUNTABLE, YOU

The moment you take responsibility for your past mistakes, your current decisions, and your plans for the future, you begin the process of taking charge of your life. That's important because if you don't take charge of your life, somebody else will. You can decide what thoughts you're going to think. You can decide what actions you're going to take. You can decide when you want to say yes or no to the opportunities and choices that come. You decide what your future will be.

People will treat you the way you treat them and the way you treat yourself (Matthew 7:12). If you are kind to yourself, people will be kind to you. If you respect yourself, people will respect you. If you want to be treated like an adult, act like an adult. How people treat you is in your hands because the law of sowing and reaping is in effect, even in relationships.

Life is a grindstone. Whether it grinds you down or polishes you up depends on what you're made of. A diamond only emerges out of intense heat and pressure. A diamond only shines with radiant brilliance after it has been under the grindstone and polished to perfection. Every diamond was once a lump of coal. What are you made of? When the heat and pressure come, when you feel the rough edge of the grindstone, will you give up and quit, or will you press back against the pressure and emerge a sparkling diamond?

You need to have the wisdom to be responsible. When you are responsible, you are able to make a response. You are "response-able." You are able to choose your response. You are not controlled by your emotions or feelings. Every problem has a solution, and you and God can find it together. So, when the problems come, don't whine about them, but shine for the glory of God (Matthew 5:14–16).

You have to take responsibility for your life and your actions. As long as you blame your problem on somebody else, you're never going to solve the problem, because as long as you give someone else the key to managing your life, you can never change directions.

Don't play the blame game. Every problem the children of Israel faced, they blamed on Moses, and the result was that God let them die in the wilderness. Stop blaming circumstances, conditions, God, or people. Stop blaming anything or everything else. The fact of the matter is that you are where you are right now. And you will stay where you are until you take responsibility for getting yourself out of where you are and into the promise and provision of God.

The fact is that you control your thoughts, you control your emotions, and you control your words. You control where you go, how you dress, what you do, how you act, and with whom you associate. You are responsible for your life, and you are responsible for you.

APPLICATION

In 1943, Winston Churchill was awarded an honorary Harvard doctorate. In his speech, he said, "The price of greatness is responsibility." [xii] You must take responsibility for your life. You become a responsible person when you admit that your choices have consequences. You are today what you decided to be yesterday. And you will be tomorrow what you decide to be today. What changes do you need to make to take responsibility for your actions, your words, and your life?

FAITH IS ACTION

Wisdom demands that you be proactive, take action, and seize the day. You've got to take charge of your life or someone else will. Christianity is a "doing" thing. The Bible says, *"faith without works is dead"* (James 2:26, NKJV). You have to go out and do something.

Christianity is putting on the whole armor of God and fighting the good fight. It is enduring hardship as a good soldier of Jesus Christ. It's not sitting around whining about the devil chasing you around. You ought to be chasing him around with the authority of the Word of God, the name of Jesus, and the power of the blood.

Christianity is doing the impossible. It's Noah building the ark when there was no rain. It is Jesus invading the temple with a whip of twisted cord, shouting, *"My house shall be called a house of prayer"* (Mark 11:17, NKJV). Christianity is faith in action. It's putting your hand to the plow and not looking back. It's running towards the giant, defeating him, and watching an entire army run in terror. It's saying, "I have a spiritual inheritance and I intend to drive the giants off because God is with me, God's favor is around me, and I will not back up, bend, bow, or turn back."

Christianity is marching around Jericho, shouting in faith until the walls come down. It's charging the gates of Hell with a water pistol, knowing that you cannot be defeated. It's Abraham walking up Mount Moriah with Isaac, believing that God will provide a lamb.

It's Samson pulling down the pillars of a temple and making his last day his best day. It's Elijah, calling fire from Heaven, surrounded by 450 false prophets of Baal. It's Peter walking on the water of the Sea of Galilee straight towards Jesus. Christianity is knowing that nothing is impossible for those who believe.

When the world comes raging, our response is to declare that God is our hope and our refuge, and we will not be ashamed. Christianity proclaims, *"I am not ashamed of the gospel, because it is the power of God that brings salvation to everyone who believes: first to the Jew, then to the Gentile"* (Romans 1:16, NIV). He is our very present help in times of need; He is the Captain of our salvation; and He is our full victory. Christ is Lord over all things.

You have everything you need. The worst thing you can do now is nothing. Do something to solve your problem. You've got to take action and make progress. God has placed the initiative inside you. Jesus said, *"Whatever you bind on earth will be bound in heaven, and whatever you loose on earth will be loosed in heaven"* (Matthew 18:18, NIV). What you do matters, and what you do makes a difference.

Engage with God in prayer. Open your Bible and read the Word of God. Lift your voice in praise. Believe on the Lord Jesus and be saved. Nothing is impossible for him who believes (Mark 9:23). Faith is action, and Christianity is a commitment to action.

APPLICATION

What does it mean for you to take action right where you are today? What plans do you need to make? What actionable steps do you need to implement?

DAY 38

REMEMBER TO REACT

A major sickness of our time is the epidemic of self-doubt. Too many Christians around the world are crippled with self-doubt, a lack of confidence, and paralyzing fear. You may have a mental blueprint of how you see yourself that was drawn by someone in your past. But you have to know that you can redraw blueprints. You can change what was and react. Blueprints are not permanent. That means you can redraw, with God's assistance, the blueprint for your future. You can force your mind and emotions to be controlled by the Word of God, not the statements of people.

No one on earth has ever lived a perfect life. But when problems come, you have to remember to react to them and not become disillusioned or disappointed with yourself. It can become easy to become resentful toward ourselves because we're less than perfect or bitter toward other people or God when life does not go our way. But the secret is that life is never going to be perfect, and when it isn't perfect, you've got to react to what wasn't perfect, so it doesn't stay that way.

A key principle to remember when you are reacting to your problems is that sometimes you will overcome your problems "little by little." Deuteronomy 7:22–23 says, *"The Lord your God will drive out those nations before you little by little; you will be unable to destroy them at once, lest the beasts of the field become too numerous for you. But the Lord your God will deliver them over to you, and will inflict defeat upon them until they are destroyed"* (NKJV). God delivered the Promised Land into the hands of Israel, "little by little," because He knew that if He completely wiped out all of the opposition in one massive bolt of lightning, they wouldn't be able to handle it. They needed to inherit the land, "little by little."

Whatever problem you're having, trust that God can solve it. If you put your hand in His, He will take care of everything. Remember that God is on your side. So, when you receive a promise from God, keep walking through the problems that come your way. Don't get bogged down in defeat, discouragement, or a "woe is me" attitude. You've got to keep your eye on the provision at the end of the road and know that when you do come into your promised land, God will be there right by your side.

As you conquer "little by little," hold fast to the joy of the Lord. In John 16:22, Jesus told His disciples that they would see Him again. In that day, *"no one will take away your joy"* (NIV). Your hope is in Jesus. You will see Him one day. Even in the middle of the problem, even when the provision seems so far away, always remember that *"the joy of the LORD is your strength"* (Nehemiah 8:10, NIV).

The joy of the Lord has nothing to do with where you are. It doesn't have to do with who you are, who you're with, what you have, or what you're going through. Paul and Silas were imprisoned with their feet in the stocks for preaching the Gospel. But when they prayed and sang hymns to God, an earthquake struck, the prison doors opened, and their chains came loose (Acts 16:22–28). No matter what you're going through, you can give the Lord a shout of praise!

APPLICATION

Read Psalm 118:24 and Philippians 4:4. What do these verses mean to you? How can you react with praise in the middle of the problems you are going through?

DAY 39

ARE YOU OBEDIENT?

Wisdom gives absolute obedience to the Word of God. When God called Jonah to preach repentance to the people of Nineveh, he not only didn't go, but he got busy going in the opposite direction. Jonah ended up in the belly of a great fish because he didn't obey God's direction. When the two angels led Lot's family out of Sodom, Lot's wife was turned into a pillar of salt because she looked back. It is important to listen to the Word of God and do what it says. Obedience could mean the difference between not only living in the wilderness or possessing the promised land, but even the difference between life and death.

You've got to learn to embrace self-mastery. Remember, it took God one day to get the Jewish people out of Egypt, but it took 40 years to get Egypt out of them. They were not able to inherit the land by faith in God, and they let their fears overtake them. In the problem, you discover who you really are.

The children of Israel saw God perform 10 mighty miracles to deliver them from Pharaoh. Then, He divided the Red Sea, rained manna from Heaven, and gave them water in the desert. And yet, they remained ungrateful for all God had done for them. Whenever God has given you something or delivered you from something, even if you don't understand it at the time, be wise enough to accept it. When you're in a problem, you need to forget what you want. Find out what God wants as quickly as possible and get busy doing that. When God says, "Listen up," say, "Yes, Lord." If God has sent you a problem to show you who you really are, start looking at yourself to see if there are any dark corners hiding in your heart. Is there anything you need to remove from your life? Because until you get your "self-life" straightened up, you're never going to have the capacity to walk into God's provision.

In Isaiah 1, the Lord said, *"'If you are willing and obedient, you shall eat the good of the land; but if you refuse and rebel, you shall be devoured by the sword'; for the mouth of the LORD has spoken"* (Isaiah 1:19–20, NKJV).

Everybody's willing to get wealth, but are you obedient? When the rich young ruler came to Jesus and asked what good deed or work he should do to inherit eternal life, Jesus said, *"If you want to be perfect, go, sell what you have and give to the poor, and you will have treasure in heaven; and come, follow Me"* (Matthew 19:21, NKJV). The young man went away sorrowful because he had great possessions. He believed in Jesus, but could he obey what Jesus asked him to do? Purpose in your heart to diligently obey the voice of the Lord your God. Jesus said, *"If you hold to my teaching, you are really my disciples"* (John 8:31, NIV). Obedience will open the doors of blessing in your life and move you out of the problem and into your promised land. What you do or do not do can impact your life forever. On the day he lost his crown, the prophet Samuel said to Saul, *"to obey is better than sacrifice"* (1 Samuel 15:22, NIV). How you react in the problem, what you believe, and what you do matters a great deal.

APPLICATION

What has the Lord called you to do? Find out what the Lord has asked of you and thoroughly organize your life around completing that assignment. Write down some steps you can take today.

DAY 40

A BLESSING FOR PROVISION

I pray this book has been a valuable resource to you as you seek God and walk with Him day by day. As you hold on to His promises with eyes firmly set upon Him, you will be able to let go of the past, walk through your problems, and move into God's provision for you.

Perhaps you are in the middle of a problem, or maybe your reaction in the problem has extended your stay in the wilderness. Maybe you have not fully taken responsibility for your life or lived in self-pity or unforgiveness for too long. Let today be the day when you draw a line in the sand of your heart, square your shoulders, and start walking hand in hand with God towards your promised land.

Today can be the day you make the decision to follow God wholeheartedly, no matter the cost. Today can be the day when you call upon the name of the Lord and receive the salvation and deliverance that only comes from Him. Today can be the day when the Lord delivers you from fear, from anxiety, from bitterness, and from unbelief. Today can be the day when you finally rest in your Savior's great arms of love.

You can take the leap of faith. You can rise up and achieve the call of God on your life. You can walk in boldness of soul and strength of spirit. You do not have to be afraid, and you do not have to cower any longer in the shadows of defeat. The Lord is a mighty warrior. The Lord is strong and mighty. The Lord is the Commander of the armies of Heaven. The Lord is His name.

Reach out to God today. Leave the wilderness behind and set your sights on God's promises for you. By faith, you can receive every spiritual blessing from Heaven and obtain a supernatural breakthrough from God's rich storehouses. By faith, you can step into a dominion of favor, defeat every giant, claim your inheritance, and prosper under the banner of the Lord of your life.

And now I pray that the Lord blesses you exceedingly and abundantly above all that you could ask, think, or imagine. May the Lord bless you and may the Lord keep you. May the Lord make His face shine upon you and may the Lord give you His peace. May God take you through the problem to the provision. May you, with bold, relentless faith, go straight through the problem and receive the promise of God. May the Lord give you the faith to experience the breakthrough that will carry you into your priceless provision, the power to walk in wisdom, and the wealth that comes to those who have conquered the self-life in the problem. And may you know the joy of the Lord that makes rich without the addition of sorrow.

Let this day and the days that follow be days of triumph and victory because God is a faithful God who will never fail you. May the Lord help you achieve your divine destiny in Him. May the Lord make a way for you where there seems to be no way. May God cause your enemies to scatter and you see them no more. May God give you victory that is only explained by the fact that a supernatural God has made it possible to live with His blessing upon your life. May God richly bless you.

APPLICATION

"The LORD bless you and keep you; the LORD make His face shine upon you, and be gracious to you; the LORD lift up His countenance upon you, and give you peace" (Numbers 6:24–26, NKJV).

"Now this *is* the commandment, *and these* are the statutes and judgments which the Lord your God has commanded to teach you, that you may observe *them* in the land which you are crossing over to possess, that you may fear the Lord your God, to keep all His statutes and His commandments which I command you, you and your son and your grandson, all the days of your life, and that your days may be prolonged. Therefore hear, O Israel, and be careful to observe *it*, that it may be well with you, and that you may multiply greatly as the Lord God of your fathers has promised you—'a land flowing with milk and honey.'

"Hear, O Israel: The Lord our God, the Lord *is* one! You shall love the Lord your God with all your heart, with all your soul, and with all your strength.

"And these words which I command you today shall be in your heart. You shall teach them diligently to your children, and shall talk of them when you sit in your house, when you walk by the way, when you lie down, and when you rise up. You shall bind them as a sign on your hand, and they shall be as frontlets between your eyes. You shall write them on the doorposts of your house and on your gates.

"So it shall be, when the Lord your God brings you into the land of which He swore to your fathers, to Abraham, Isaac, and Jacob, to give you large and beautiful cities which you did not build, houses full of all good things, which you did not fill, hewn-out wells which you did not dig, vineyards and olive trees which you did not plant—when you have eaten and are full—*then* beware, lest you forget the Lord who brought you out of the land of Egypt, from the house of bondage. You shall fear the Lord your God and serve Him, and shall take oaths in His name."

Deuteronomy 6:1–13 (NKJV)

John Hagee is the founder and senior pastor of Cornerstone Church in San Antonio, Texas, a nondenominational evangelical church with more than 22,000 active members. He is the author of more than forty books, including several *New York Times* Bestsellers, his latest being *Earth's Last Empire: The Final Game of Thrones*. Pastor Hagee is the founder and chairman of Christians United for Israel (CUFI), with over one million members. Hagee Ministries television and radio outreach spans America and the nations of the world.

To learn more about Pastor John Hagee, visit:

Hagee Ministries:
jhm.org

Facebook
HageeMinistries

Twitter
PastorJohnHagee
HageeMinistries

Instagram
PastorJohnHagee
HageeMinistries

END NOTES

i   Susan Martin Millers, *Jim Elliot Missionary Martyr*, (Uhrichsville, Barbour Publishing, 1996)

ii   Eric Metaxes, *Amazing Grace, William Wilberforce and the Heroic Campaign to End Slavery*, (New York, HarperOne, An Imprint of HarperCollinsPublishers, 2007)

iii   https://www.westminster-abbey.org/abbey-commemorations/commemorations/david-livingstone

iv   https://winstonchurchill.org/

v   https://ourrabbijesus.com/articles/a-good-eye-or-a-bad-eye-a-cryptic-but-critical-idiom/

vi   https://www.pewresearch.org/fact-tank/2018/04/27/about-one-third-of-u-s-children-are-living-with-an-unmarried-parent/

vii   https://medlineplus.gov/ency/patientinstructions/000355.htm#:~:text=Most%20American%20children%20spend%20about,child%20to%20sleep%20at%20night

viii   https://hymnary.org/text/o_soul_are_you_weary_and_troubled

iv   John Bunyan, *The Pilgrim's Progress* (New Jersey, Jove Publications, Inc., for Fleming H. Revell Company, 1980), 39

x   David Wilkerson, *The Cross and the Switchblade* (New York, The Berkley Publishing Group, Published by Penguin Group (USA), Inc, 1962), 7

xi   Viktor Frankl, *Man's Search for Meaning* (Boston, Beacon Press, 1959)

xii   https://winstonchurchill.org/